W9-CMD-970

Received   4-25-67   JE

BOOKS BY ALLAN W. ECKERT

THE GREAT AUK

A TIME OF TERROR

THE SILENT SKY

WILD SEASON

WILD SEASON

WILD SEASON

BY ALLAN W. ECKERT

WITH ILLUSTRATIONS BY
Karl E. Karalus

LITTLE, BROWN AND COMPANY · BOSTON · TORONTO

Published simultaneously in Canada
by Little, Brown & Company (Canada) Limited

PRINTED IN THE UNITED STATES OF AMERICA

For my son
Joseph Matthew Eckert

. . . with the heartfelt wish that he may,
in the lifetime which lies ahead of him,
learn the love and respect for nature in
all its forms that has so enriched his
father's life . . .

WILD SEASON

PROLOGUE

Newly wakened from its eons-long slumber, the glacier had become a hungry monster ponderously grinding its way across a defenseless land. Its frosted teeth sank deeply into the earth in a hundred, a thousand, a hundred thousand individual bites. Its appetite was immense and in its gullet the ingested forests and fields, hills and dunes were masticated by great round granite boulders.

One day this irresistible mass of ice would come to be known as the Labradorean Sheet, but for now it was merely a great glacier which gnawed its way southward out of its bleak northern lair, eating the land and drinking the rivers of the land, and its appetite was immense.

But even such an appetite as this had its limitations and when — in the area that would eventually come to be known as Wisconsin and Illinois — the glacier overestimated its own capacity, it ground to a halt, seemed to ponder its limitations for an era, as it perspired mightily under a warming sun, and then retreated toward the far north to resume hibernation.

As it grudgingly withdrew, it left behind its fertile droppings of pulverized and digested trees and rocks, sand and soil in a massive blanket over the land. And in those places where it had bitten deep gouges from the earth, it relieved itself of the rivers it had drunk. The gouges were filled to the level of the land with a muddy liquid which gradually cleared as the suspended particles of matter slowly settled upon the unhealed bottom.

In the centuries that passed, the ice sheet was forgotten. New forests and grasses grew with swiftness and strength in the rich black loam which was the offal of the glacier, and they surrounded the multitude of water-filled bites taken out of the earth, and these bodies of water came to be called lakes.

Near the line that separates the states of Wisconsin and Illinois is one of these glacial lakes. It is a small one as such lakes go, and its shoreline is cloaked with deep woods in which there are scattered pines and cedars, but mostly consisting of hardwoods: elms and hickories, walnuts and maples and oaks. It would have been a circular lake except for a bay of some two hundred acres or more which interrupts the northwestern arc of the shoreline. Here there is shallow water over deep mucky soil, and much of the water surface is clad in swamp grasses and bulrushes, reeds and lily pads, and here too there are several small low-lying islands visited only by wildlife and occasional fishermen and waterfowl hunters.

The greater portion of the lake's circular shoreline — perhaps four miles or so — is principally sandy. There are occasional small marshy areas, as well as several muddy and rocky stretches, but mostly the shoreline is hard-packed sand.

This lake has a personality all its own and a variety of moods — such moods usually predicated upon the whims of weather. More often than not in the early morning or late evening hours it lies quietly, its surface as flat and reflective as a mirror, dimpled occasionally by the rise of a feeding fish, the plunge of a submerging loon or the protrusion of a turtle's head. On bright days when a gentle breeze stirs, the lake is an inviting blue pool a mile and a half across, chuckling softly at some secret humor shared with the shoreline. But on gray, stormy days it pulls the cloud cover over itself, hiding the blue, and heaves restlessly, sometimes crying out in foamy protest as the wind tugs at its surface.

This is Oak Lake.

In its clear waters and lush marshes, along its shores and in the verdant woods and fields which border it, there lives a vast and varied population of wildlife. No creature here is not in large measure dependent upon other creatures of its own or other species for survival; and no creature here does not give of itself — even if ultimately it be by death — to the continuance of the whole natural scheme of things.

That is the way of nature, and nature is firm in her ways. There is no pity here, no mercy, but neither is there malice or hatred. There is violence and harshness, but there is also serenity and great beauty. And though there is death, so too there is abundant life, for in nature death is necessarily a part of life.

At Oak Lake, as elsewhere in natural environs, there is a purpose to all things and among all creatures: there is purpose in being born and in living; there is purpose in reproducing and in the raising of young; there is purpose even in death, for while death among wild creatures in nature may be harsh and unexpected, it is, unlike death in man, rarely tragic, rarely needless and never wasteful.

With the arrival of a warm new spring at Oak

Lake, the wildlife population is enlarged by the arrival of many birds that have wintered far to the south and by the reappearance of numerous mammals, reptiles and amphibians that have for long months been hibernating in deep seclusion.

This year, as in most years, the bitter grip of winter relaxed in late March, and April was a month of transition, a month of raw winds and frigid rains, a month of weather which gradually tempered as the weeks slipped away. But it is the month of May that has brought the warmth of true spring, filling the creatures in and around the lake with a new energy and a sort of exultation for the very act of living during this season. For spring is a season of growth and life; it is a season of mating and nesting and rearing young; it is a season of seeking prey and avoiding predators; it is a season of living and it is a season of dying.

And most of all, it is a wild season.

I

THE FIRST DAY
OF MAY

A LONG Oak Lake's shoreline where the sandy banks
gave way to mud and the large marshy bay
began, new green blades of cattail reeds were just
beginning to knife through the water surface close
to shore. They were dwarfed by the dry, dun-colored
stalks and foliage of last year's growth still standing.

Within a month these little shoots would tower in
emerald splendor above the wind-lashed, crooked
remnants of their forebears, forming a two-hundred-
acre sea of reeds; but at their present stage they were
only barely visible. It was remarkable how clearly the
line of cattail growth was drawn, abruptly springing
from the water in a veritable wall, for where the mud
of the marsh gave way to the sandy bottom of the
lake proper, the reeds did not grow.

It was in this area, along the perimeter of the reed growth a few feet from shore, that the sandy mud beneath three feet of clear water abruptly stirred, although the reason for its faint jiggling was not at once apparent. A little plume of silt blossomed slowly upward in the water with a smokelike billowing, began to dissipate and then was followed by a second and third plume, each larger and more disrupting than its predecessor.

A smooth webbed foot came into view momentarily, retracted beneath the mud and then reappeared. Suddenly there was a larger commotion as a small bullfrog freed itself, kicked rather sluggishly underwater toward the shore and pulled itself from the water onto a floating platform of matted reed debris. It blinked slowly a few times and the warm sun glinted brightly on the wetness of its sides and back. Its throat swelled hesitantly with the first air it had inhaled since early last October when it had selected this particular spot to enter hibernation.

This was the little bullfrog's fourth spring, but his first emergence from hibernation as a fully formed frog. He had hatched from an expansive jellylike egg mass containing nearly twenty thousand eggs which had been deposited among the reeds only a dozen yards from here. His first two years after hatching had been spent as a tadpole; in summer, feeding upon green algae along with bits of aquatic plant and animal residue in the oozes of the marshy shoreline fringe; in winter, hibernating beneath the mud in this same general area.

Last summer had come his metamorphosis. He had emerged from his second hibernation as an oversized tadpole fully six inches long, and in a matter of weeks he had begun to sprout hind legs. His eyes had changed markedly, growing larger and more pro-tuberant, and his mouth had become wider, to ac-commodate a diet expanded to include small aquatic insects.

By midsummer both his hind and front legs were fully formed — the rear feet webbed but the front more like smoothly fingered hands — and the long tail was beginning to weaken, preparatory to falling off. The brownish, yellow-speckled color he had worn as a tadpole was disappearing and his back was becoming a deep green, his stomach and the under-sides of his legs like the color of old ivory.

That he was a male frog was evident by the tym-panum, or ear — a large circle of membrane just behind and below his eye. It was slightly larger than the eye and this was the single external sex-identifying factor; in the female frog the tympanum is always smaller than the eye.

His development had continued through the late summer months and he began to spend more time out of the water than in it, catching a variety of insects to appease his ever-present hunger. And when, during the second week of October, he had chosen this location to make his final dive of the year and burrow into the loose bottom to await the coming of spring, no vestige of tail, no trace of his tadpole existence remained evident.

He was smaller this spring, in total length, than he had been last year at this time as a tadpole. His squat body was not much over two inches long and even with his hind legs fully outstretched he was still not quite five inches. It would take several years more for him to reach full adult size and another few years or more beyond that before he became a truly huge "granddaddy" bullfrog with a body upwards of eight inches long and great muscular hind legs another ten inches in length beyond that. And he might live to the ripe old age of eighteen or twenty years.

That, of course, was if he survived. But the odds against such survival were high, as they had been ever since his hatching. In fact, of the twoscore thousand other tadpoles that had hatched along with him from that single egg mass, less than two hundred had managed to survive to see this fourth spring. Weather, predators and, in some cases, disease had destroyed the rest.

In nature there is little margin for miscalculation, and already the little bullfrog had made a serious error in boldly clambering out of the water onto the floating debris and exposing himself so clearly. The decaying material upon which he sat was a dark, dirty brown in color and his own greenish body, not yet mottled with the gray and brown markings of the adult frog, was not at all well camouflaged against such a background. And instead of sitting with his head held low, he perched with his snout raised and the cream-colored throat, which would become a deeper yellow in time, appeared now like a tiny beacon pulsing rhythmically with his breathing.

The little bullfrog blinked rapidly several times in succession and then sat very still, instinctively alert, as he would always be, for anything edible which might come swimming, crawling or flying within his range. His large bright eyes missed little. Six feet away a big dragonfly hovered over the weathered remains of a fluffy brown cattail still protruding from the water, though now at a rather unnatural angle. The insect alighted for only an instant and then shot away in a blur of speed, a faint rattling sound coming from its clear wings. Closer at hand, behind him, a honeybee landed on the shore an inch from the water, crawled gingerly to the edge to drink and then it too buzzed off. The frog had seen them both but he had not moved.

Nor had the great blue heron.

Eight feet away from where the young frog had come out of the water the large bird stood motionless on girderlike legs in water no more than six inches deep. Had it been standing erect it would have been about five feet tall, but it had frozen in a somewhat hunched, imbalanced position as the bullfrog had emerged from the water, and now its intent gaze was directed at this amphibian.

The bird had been in the process of taking a step when the frog appeared, and now it stood with one foot arrested in the air just above the water and its weight leaning rather precariously forward. Slowly, so slowly that the movement was not discernible, not even to the little bullfrog patiently watching for movement, the foot lowered ahead of the other leg, easily slipped back into the water without causing a ripple or sound, and the weight of the bird gradually shifted to this new purchase. It took a quarter-hour

to complete that single step, but it closed the gap
between bird and frog to less than seven feet. Already the trailing foot was leaving the bottom and
rising just as slowly as the opposite foot had
lowered.

This heron was a majestic bird, exhibiting an awesome sort of beauty. Its huge wings, tightly folded
now, were generally slate-colored, a rather deep bluish gray; the neat pinion feathers were darker, practically black, and the leading edge of the wings was a
rich chestnut hue. The bird's forehead, crown and
cheeks were white, melding into a faint bluish tint at
the neck, and a slash of black feathering began over
each eye, merged at the back of the head and formed
a trailing crest of long black plumes. Even longer
individual plumes of gray hung from its breast. Its
gray lower throat was scattered with white, black and
rusty-colored streakings and its stomach plumage
was black interspersed with reddish and white streaking.

But this bird's most arresting feature was the
unwavering yellow eye above an evenly tapered sti-
letto of a beak over six inches long. Both eye and
beak were aimed, at this moment, directly at the little
green bullfrog.

The heron's foot that was behind had now cleared

the surface, inched forward and soundlessly, without rippling, entered the water again ahead of the other leg. The distance separating them was now five feet and, imperceptibly as it continued the forward movement, the heron cocked its head for the strike, bending its neck into a squashed S-shape, as.if it were a great spring ready to be triggered.

To within a fraction of an inch the heron knew when to strike. Regardless of whether the bird's target was frog, fish or crayfish, or even a mouse or gopher — rodents upon which it frequently dined — it rarely missed its prey, and it was dangerously close to the striking point now.

At this moment another creature entered the scene. While the heron's sharp gaze never strayed from the frog, it became aware that a mayfly nymph had attached itself to the pile of debris only an inch beneath the surface and several inches to the far side of the frog.

Though still unconscious of its own looming peril, the little bullfrog was also keenly aware of the slight movement to his right and he shifted position minutely, watching intently as the nymph crept up a small stem. Unconcernedly the insect emerged from the water and stopped a short distance above the surface. Here it would cling until its outer skin dried

enough in the sun to split down the back and allow it to emerge as an adult mayfly and ultimately fly away when its wings spread and hardened in the air.

As the frog kept his own gaze locked on the nymph and tensed his legs beneath him, the final slow step of the heron had been taken and the bird's body leaned forward to the critical point. There was a moment of time balanced, an instant of utter stillness, and then several things happened simultaneously. The little bullfrog, still oblivious of the greater peril, leaped to snatch the mayfly just a fractional instant before the rapier beak of the heron shot forward. By the slimmest of margins the point of the bird's beak missed impaling the frog's body and jabbed deeply into the debris pile.

The terrifying realization of his own danger struck the frog in mid-jump and he twisted violently, the nymph forgotten. As he struck the water two sharp kicks of his hind legs drove him to the bottom and he slipped neatly beneath a layer of decaying plant matter, burrowing in deeply. Then he became still.

Above him the heron recovered itself, shook its head with two quick little jerks, as if in agitation, and then emitted a grating, guttural cry which carried far across the water. It paused for a moment and then leaped upward into ponderous yet beautiful flight, its long legs trailing straight behind.

For two or three minutes the little bullfrog remained quiet, and when at last he did move, it was with extreme caution, picking his way slowly through the debris closer to shore until, under a protective covering of floating reed blades, he inched his head above the surface. He was well hidden, yet able to see and breathe, and he remained in this position for a considerable while.

Nature rarely tolerates carelessness in wild creatures, and few opportunities are given for a second chance. The lesson had been a frightful and very nearly fatal one, and it had been well learned. Not again would the little bullfrog boldly climb out of the water as he had done at first, nor would he again be so indiscriminate in choosing a background upon which to couch himself for any length of time.

At last, with continued caution, he raised himself until he was mostly out of the water and his eyes carefully scanned his surroundings for potential danger. Less than ten feet away a painted turtle, seven inches across the shell, was just climbing out of the water onto a thick branch protruding at an angle, there to sun himself. The frog knew instinc-

tively that no danger to himself existed here so long
as he kept a safe distance from the reptile's head.

A little farther away a huge adult male bullfrog
sat quietly in these shallows, its upper back and head
clear of the water. As the little frog watched he saw
yet another bullfrog, a female about his own size,
leap from her heretofore hidden position near the
big frog in pursuit of a damselfly. The dainty, iri-
descent-green, black-winged insect flitted to rest at
the end of a cattail blade which dipped close to shore.
The leap carried the small female to within striking
distance of the insect and her long tongue shot out
and snatched it up with great accuracy. The damselfly was in her mouth before her jump ended.

But the leap had also carried her within range of a
danger she had not at all anticipated. The huge male
bullfrog suddenly lunged forward, caught the
smaller frog deftly and clamped his wide mouth shut,
leaving her legs still kicking frenziedly outside. For
several minutes it sat thus until the struggles of the
smaller frog weakened and then it lowered its head
and used handlike front feet to stuff the twitching
legs into its mouth, too. In another moment the little
female had been swallowed.

Thoroughly alarmed by the drama, the little male
frog now carefully slipped away from this area and

took up a new position twenty feet or more farther away, where a little pocket of water indented the shoreline. Here he sat for several hours as daylight faded. He caught a few insects, using an economy of movement common to his species, but they eased his hunger only temporarily and it wasn't until just before full darkness had fallen that he spied a crayfish not much smaller than himself poking about in the shallowest portion of the miniature cove. Two swift leaps took him to it and he caught it up and swallowed it at once, oblivious of its size and hardness and potentially dangerous pincers.

For some minutes afterward he could feel the crustacean moving within him, and it was really not an unpleasant sensation. But the process of digestion was rapid, the digestive juices powerful, and soon all inner movement ceased and the little frog basked in a sort of pleasant stupor as the flesh of the crayfish nourished him.

The sounds of the marsh at night were numerous, to which now and again he added a rather tremulous and high-pitched croaking little like the great sonorous rumblings of the adult bullfrogs. But mostly he just sat and listened, knowing, without even realizing he knew, the size and sex of any particular bullfrog croaking. And strangely, when the croak was that from a female, particularly one of about his own size, a little well of excitement stirred in him.

From not too far away among the outer reeds there came a swirling splash as some sort of predatory fish — probably a largemouth bass or chain pickerel — snatched its prey. Once, some time after dark, a duck quacked sleepily a long way off, and there were several occasions when sudden fear stabbed him as heard but unseen wings fluttered past close over his head.

The night grew progressively cooler, and several times the small bullfrog shifted position to settle himself deeper in the water, which was now warmer than the air. Soon only his eyes, tympanum and nostrils remained above the water, and in this position he stayed for the rest of the night.

II

THE SECOND DAY OF MAY

B Y dawn, with all remnants of the crayfish gone from his stomach, the little bullfrog was hungry again, and in rapid succession he caught several damselflies and numerous mayflies made somewhat lethargic by the cool night air.

He began to travel along the shoreline away from the marsh, and though he didn't hop very rapidly he moved along in a reasonably steady series of jumps and soon had covered a respectable distance. He reached a point where the bank of Oak Lake became quite steep, and remaining on the relatively level ground took him before long to a position several feet above the water. The dew-drenched grasses here were young and fresh, containing a variety of insect life. He fed rapidly and well, rarely missing a strike and stuffing his own stomach until it was swelled tight and firm.

Already he had come thirty yards or more from where he had emerged yesterday from hibernation, and the ground here was much more solid, covered with a new growth of land plants rather than aquatics or marsh growth. There were trees here, too, the first he had ever been close to, and the base of each of these he found to be a good hunting ground for smaller insects. Ants, spiders, flies, bees, caterpillars and other invertebrates seemed drawn to them, and as he crouched beneath one tree a little black ground beetle lumbered nonchalantly toward him. He watched its approach attentively and when it was within catching distance he leaped forward and snapped it in.

At once a nauseous material filled his mouth and the accompanying stench was sickening. Hastily he spat out the offensive insect, which, only a little the worse for wear, wobbled away into the undergrowth. The frog clawed at his mouth and tongue with his front feet and his eyes blinked rapidly. After a moment he regurgitated the residue of insects from his stomach, but still the terrible taste and burning remained.

At length, his eyes smarting and skin badly irritated by the fluid the ground beetle had ejected, the little bullfrog leaped to the edge of the bank, poised there a moment and then dived into the water. He kicked his way to the sandy bottom, which was deeper here than along the marshy shoreline, and rubbed his body in the bottom grit, then even scooped up a mouthful and spat it out. He scraped along the bottom all the way back to shore and then headed for a little clump of blossoming water grass growing out of inch-deep water. Another lesson had been learned: certain smaller creatures than he possessed powerful weapons, and he would not again strike at little black beetles lest they be armed with such a noxious defense.

He reached the clump of water grass without incident and pushed his way into it a short distance, where he discovered a tiny clearing no more than a foot in diameter. It was ideal for hunting and he assumed a stationary pose on one side of it. His own coloration blended almost exactly with that of the grasses and, except for the sharpest scrutiny, he was so well camouflaged as to be invisible. A number of the tiny pale blue blossoms ringed the little clearing and there was every likelihood that insects attracted to their nectar might fall prey to the accuracy of his long tongue.

The fact that he was so well hidden was most fortunate for him. He had been sitting there for nearly an hour, dining occasionally on small flies, when a faint rasping sound reached his ears; he became sharply alert, maintaining his immobility, yet ready to jump away in an instant if it became necessary.

The sound drew nearer, and abruptly a sinister head poked into the clearing of the weed clump. The little bullfrog's throat stopped pulsing as he held his breath, but his heartbeat speeded greatly at the distinct threat posed by this intruder.

It was a water snake, large, ugly and extremely dangerous to a frog of his size. With almost any other enemy he could have leaped away, dived to the bottom and found safety, but not from such a predator as this. The snake could swim as fast or even faster than he and could follow him practically anyplace he went. His only hope lay in keeping still and remaining undetected by the serpent's keen senses.

The snake swiveled its head back and forth as its forked tongue flicked out smoothly and tested the air for spoor. What little movement of air was here was coming from the snake toward the frog and so that sensitive organ did not detect him. Nevertheless, the snake's eyesight was sharp enough that even the slightest movement by the little frog could be seen, and so he remained absolutely still.

In a moment the fierce head disappeared into another portion of the clump and the snake continued on its way. Though the length of the reptile was only three and a half feet, it seemed to take an interminable time for that body to pass and the little frog watched in fearful fascination. Quite thick and heavily scaled, the body of the snake was a general medium brown in color with darker brown splotches and bands across the back and sides. The fact that its skin was unusually clear and bright indicated that it had only recently shed, for normally its hide was dingy and the markings almost hidden by an overall drabness. Gradually the long body slid past, its diameter dwindling as the tail grew nearer. And then, as suddenly as it had come, the water snake was gone.

For the better part of an hour afterward the small bullfrog maintained his same frozen position, breathing very shallowly, paying no attention to insects which hovered or alighted nearby and listening in-

tently for any sound of the snake's return. At length
he moved slowly to the edge of the weed clump,
peered out and saw no sign of danger.

But there was something which caught and held
his gaze, and he hopped several times along the shore
until he came even with a large log which lay parallel
to the waterline, half buried in the sand. On the lake
side of the log the water was rather deep, but the
uppermost part of the wood projected above the
surface — a strip of dry bark perhaps five inches
wide. And waddling along this strip as if it were a
bumpy little highway was what had initially
attracted the little frog's attention — a glossy
brown May beetle.

Two hops more put the bullfrog onto the log and
for a short span of time he sat there quietly watching, studying not only the beetle but equally scanning the shore, water and sky for possible danger to
himself. He was learning rapidly the little tricks of
survival. When he had satisfied himself that no danger was evident, he hopped twice again and came
within reach of the beetle, which was about the size of
a rather small acorn.

The insect had by this time encountered a stubby
branch rising from the log and climbed it to a point
where it was broken off, about seven inches above the

log. Here it sat in apparent puzzlement, its short
antennae waving gently. A crack widened down its
back and the leathery underwings began to unfurl
for flight. In that instant the little bullfrog below
leaped and neatly snatched it from the perch.

The jump carried the frog out into the water
twelve or fourteen inches from the log, and for a
moment after splashing into it he bobbed carelessly
on the surface as he concentrated on swallowing the
beetle. It was the second major mistake the young
frog had made since leaving hibernation.

A deep shadow, until now invisible in the shade of
the log under the water's surface, separated from its
hiding place and drifted outward, revealing itself to
be a largemouth bass over a foot and a half in length
and weighing perhaps three pounds. The fish angled
upward toward the frog, approaching almost casually, and not until it was eight inches away did the
little bullfrog comprehend the danger and thrust
himself frantically toward the log.

It was a futile effort. With a single flip of its
powerful tail, the bass overtook the frog, engulfed it
in its huge mouth as it broke the surface and
splashed water all over the projecting portion of the
log.

The fish arrowed away toward deeper waters, swallowing as it swam, and the swirl it had made on the surface spread out in expanding rings, which gradually faded away until the water was once again calm.

*   *   *

The largemouth bass cruised slowly along the bottom into the deeper waters of Oak Lake after swallowing the little bullfrog. That tidbit, coming on top of two crayfish, an inch-long bluegill and a large hornyhead chub minnow, had satisfied her hunger and now she would rest for a time.

She was a creature of habit, this bass, and the half-sunken log along the shoreline was a morning feeding place to which she came on a relatively regular basis. By nature she preferred a rather sedentary existence, exerting herself in the pursuit of food to some extent in the morning and evening hours, but during the daylight hours and much of the night remaining motionless alongside some sunken log or rock or clump of water plants, or else slowly and more or less aimlessly cruising the waters of her Oak Lake domain.

She was, at this period, a bit more lethargic than usual, for within her were some twelve thousand eggs in various stages of development. Not all of these would be laid at once, for it was nature's way of protecting the species to have her lay only a portion of them at a time, spaced over a period of several weeks, thereby insuring the continuation of the species should one mass of spawn chance to be wiped out.

Within a few minutes after devouring the bullfrog she was moving along very slowly about fifty feet from shore in water twelve feet deep. Long, gently swaying fronds of water weeds — tape grass, hornwort, cabomba and water milfoil — rose from the bottom in surrealistic forests having numerous aisles and clearings through which the bass drifted casually. A variety of small water life — tiny freshwater shrimp, snails, insect nymphs, minnows, little sunfish and bluegills and other creatures — clung close to the protection the water growth afforded and stared at the passing bass fearfully, but the bass paid little attention to them.

The route she followed now was one she had taken often. Several hundred yards away the rotted and waterlogged hulk of an old rowboat was mired in the bottom, and it was beside this wreck that she spent much of her time, fanning the water quietly several inches off the bottom and rarely moving away from it unless some smaller fish or crayfish was so foolish as to swim within range and tempt her into an abrupt, slashing atack.

Lying so still in the short water weeds beside the hulk and well hidden in its deep shadow, she was very nearly invisible. Her own dark green coloration on top and light belly camouflaged her perfectly. A series of black blotches patterned her back and were repeated in a broad irregular line down the length of each side from gill plate to tail. Except for a still incompletely healed gash across her back just in front of the dorsal fin, it was unlikely that any passing creature would spot her.

This sunken hulk was in the center of what she considered her territory, and it was an area she guarded well, chasing away any intruder she felt was encroaching. The self-appointed sentry duty was, in essence, her greatest activity during the day, for invariably there would be intruders: long, alligator-snouted gars, lazily meandering carp, an occasional scavenging bowfin and now and then an exploring turtle. In fact, about the only moving creatures she ignored entirely were the snails moving slowly on the boat hulk or in the vegetation and the large clams which pushed themselves laboriously across the bottom with a single muscular foot, leaving long serpentine trails behind them.

But this time when she approached her territory she found it occupied by another largemouth bass, a male not much smaller than herself. His tail and ventral fins were curiously inflamed and ragged, but this did not concern her as she tensed her muscles to slash at him and drive him away as she had done with many another bass that had encroached here. Yet, something in his manner gave her pause this time. For one thing, he showed none of the apparent reluctance of the others at her approach. Instead he began angling toward her, picked up speed and then began circling her as she slowed. When it appeared she would stop, he bumped her side with his snout and gradually began moving her toward shallower water. She let him guide her, but only grudgingly. Every now and then she would balk and at such times his onslaughts would become more vigorous, more determined, and he would nip her side or gill plate and drive her on.

And then, in water no more than four feet deep, they reached his destination. Here a saucer-shaped declivity about two feet in diameter had been constructed in the bottom by the male; this was why his tail and underfins were in such reddened and tattered condition. It had taken him many hours to carry away bottom debris and then use his fins to fan this little area clear of loose sand and expose the bed of gravel beneath.

Even now, apparently detecting more sand or sediment that had settled atop the newly cleaned area since his departure, he left the female's side and darted to the declivity, fanning the bottom so vigorously with tail and fins that several times he was almost lying on his side.

This was the nesting area he had built — a construction called a redd. It was here that he meant for the female to lay her eggs, but the larger fish was curiously disinterested. As the male continued his energetic sweeping of the redd, she blandly drifted off and headed back toward her own special territory.

She had not gone very far when the male realized she was leaving. With a heavy thrust of his tail he caught up to her and drove her back. Still unsatisfied with the condition of the redd, he resumed his fanning action, and once again the female slowly cruised away. Thrice this same sequence was reenacted, but at length the female gave in and gradually moved over and positioned herself a few inches above the freshly cleaned gravel.

For a long time she held herself in position with faint movement of her pectoral fins, and then her rear quarter settled until her tail was resting on the smooth little stones. Her body abruptly contracted and expanded in several convulsive spasms, and a stream of bright orange roe — eggs each about the size of the head of a pin — spurted from her vent and coated much of the redd in a sticky blanket which adhered wherever it touched. Three, four, five times more she deposited streams of roe and then, finished, raised herself from the bottom and drifted slightly away from the bed.

During this laying process the male had grown decidedly nervous. He circled the redd and the female numerous times, occasionally darting off to one side or another to frighten away a curious passing blue-gill or sunfish or small bass. When the third series of eggs had been deposited he stopped close to the fringe of the nest, not moving any of his fins, and let himself drift to the bottom. The drift took him about half an inch farther from the nest, so he swam to the other side and performed the same action.

Satisfied that he had correctly estimated the slight water movement, he now began his most important function. Even while the female was still laying, he sprayed from his own vent a gush of cloudy white material called milt. It fogged the water and gradually settled over the nesting area. Twice more he did this, from slightly different positions, while the female continued laying; and when she finished and moved off the nest he took her position directly over the eggs and two times again clouded the water with milt. The brightness of the eggs was now somewhat dulled by the fine coating of sperm-heavy milt that had settled over them.

With this fertilization process completed, the male turned his attention back to the female, but now his attitude had undergone a marked change. He became sharply aggressive, thrusting his snout into her side and biting savagely at her. He deliberately struck the unhealed gash on her back, and she flinched badly. A flip of her tail carried her a short distance away, but not enough to suit him, and he followed doggedly, bumping and biting her, concentrating on irritating her injury until at last he had forced her back into the water-weed corridors. Then he returned to the redd and began circling it nervously, guarding the spawn against any possible harm. He would continue to do so until the eggs hatched in three to six days.

When the eggs did hatch, the tiny fry with little yolk sacs attached to their bellies would hide at once in the gravel crevices and remain there for a day or so until the yolk had been absorbed. And during all this time the male would continue to guard them. But when they emerged as tiny black fry hardly an inch long they would have to scatter rapidly, for by then

his protectiveness would have disappeared and his
hunger would be intense and he would devour all he
could catch. Those fry that escaped would hide
among the water weeds and feed there on the minute
animals called cyclops and daphnia until they were
large enough to begin catching insects and other
aquatic life slightly larger.

But with all this the female was wholly unconcerned. Tired now from her exertions in depositing
the roe, she cruised casually back to her sunken boat
and took up a well-hidden position alongside it. In a
few days or a week from now perhaps a different male
would drive her to another nest to repeat the process,
but for the time being she would remain alone.

During the rest of this day she relaxed beside the
old boat hulk, moving away from its bulk only once
to chase off a small chain pickerel that had entered
the clearing. But when evening came she grew rest-
less and, with one final circling of the clearing, she
moved off toward shore.

She was very alert now, watching for any creature
she might catch as food. Several times she blundered
too close to bass nesting areas and the males guarding these redds dashed angrily at her; she easily
swerved away from them, knowing they never chased

anything very far from the bed lest another intruder approach from the other side.

At length she came to a natural channel paralleling the shore. It was deep — perhaps six or seven feet — and a dozen feet from shore. The channel itself was only eight or ten feet wide, and on the lake side it quickly shallowed out again to a smooth sandy expanse two or three feet deep. It was along the ledge of the channel closest to shore that she now swam slowly. At once she spied a large crayfish moving into the shallows to shed. Its tough outer shell was already loose and ready to be shucked off to expose the soft shell beneath.

A flashing dart, and she had scooped it up and swallowed it and continued on her way without pause. But though the hunting had begun in a promising manner, it did not remain good. A few more crayfish were seen but they managed to thrust backward through the water into the sanctuary of dense water weeds or under rocks. Several times she spurted after bluegills up to four or five inches in length but they flicked away in terror and hid themselves in the heavy vegetation cover until she had gone on.

A squadron of smaller bass, seven of them, were now following her closely but watching her very carefully. She would unhesitatingly grab one of them,

the largest of which was only a half-pound in weight,
if any came too close. But they had learned that a
bass of her size slashing into a school of minnows or
little bluegills often frightened the smaller fish so
badly that they became confused, and in attempting
to escape her would run right into them and be easily
caught.

But both minnows and bluegills were staying uncommonly close to cover this evening, and, though
the channel she was following paralleled the shoreline
for over a quarter-mile, by the time she reached the
end of it she had managed to catch only one very
small sunfish and a May beetle that she spotted kicking weakly on the surface.

At the end of the channel she paused and rested, a
faint memory stirring her of danger in the shallows
stretching out beyond this point. Only a week ago she
had fed here in the early morning light and had not
stopped when she reached the end of the channel.
Instead, she had continued out into those shallows,
from which projected the onionlike tops of new bulrush growth in water no more than a foot deep. Here
the hunting was good and she had fed well on crayfish and minnows until suddenly a shadow had
crossed her and instinctively she lunged to one side.

It was well she did so.

Few times in its plunge from the heights at a fish had the osprey ever missed its mark, but that time it did. From an altitude of seventy feet it had hurtled downward toward the bass in the shallows. At only six feet over the water it had thrust out its great five-foot wings and spread its talons wide to snatch the bass, but the sudden spurt of the fish had moved her away just enough. One outstretched talon had raked across her back and turned her completely over, but by the time the bird had recovered itself, the bass was streaking back toward the channel as fast as she had ever swum, a great V-wake following her until the deeper waters of the channel were reached.

The injury was serious enough but not fatal and in several weeks it would be healed. But the niggling memory of danger in those shallows remained, and so now the female turned and headed back to retrace her course through the channel. The trip back was even less profitable than coming, and only one very small crayfish fell prey to her. By the time she reached the other end of the channel it had become quite dark out, and she continued to cruise toward the marsh through water only several feet deep.

At the beginning of the area where the sandy bottom turned to mud and reed growth became plentiful she stopped abruptly and remained poised, ready to flee. Some twenty or thirty feet away from her she had detected another female largemouth bass. It was a huge fish, weighing just a little over eight pounds. She did not actually see the bigger bass except as a dark smudge moving against a darker background, but the sensitivity of her lateral line identified it for her every bit as clearly as eyesight in bright daylight could have.

The lateral line was a row of keenly vibration-sensitive scales which ran from gill plate to tail on each side of her body. All fish had such an organ as this and depended upon it not only in seeking out food, especially at night, but in detecting and identifying enemies. So sensitive was it that just the vibrations the larger bass made as it cruised slowly along told her not only what size fish it was but that it was of her own species. And more than once these lateral line sensors had directed her from as far distant as fifty or sixty feet away on a moonless night to a beetle or moth or little frog struggling along on the surface of the water.

She remained very still until the larger bass had gone out of range into the deeper area of the marshy bay, and then she angled closer toward shore and leisurely cruised among the old stems and newly emerging shoots of cattail reed and bulrush, pond-weed and sweet flag, pickerel weed and water lily.

It was in the area of water lily growth that she encountered good hunting again, and in quick succession she caught three small frogs. Her appetite temporarily satisfied, she rested beside a rotting stump sticking from the water. Digestion was rapid in her system, however, and within an hour she was actively on the prowl again.

At one point, near the edge of the cattail growth where the water was just over four feet deep, she paused as she had done frequently before to see if her lateral line sensors detected anything. This time she was rewarded.

A yearling bass only seven inches long was moving along nervously quite close to the cattail cover, ready to take shelter at once if danger loomed, or to dart in pursuit of prey if any was detected. The larger female remained motionless as the yearling approached, but it was still twenty feet from her concealed position when there was a sudden commotion.

A large snapping turtle hidden on the bottom had also been aware of the smaller fish's approach, and had remained rocklike until the bass began to pass only inches in front of its head. With incredible speed the turtle's head shot forward and its sharp beak snapped, but its aim was not as good as it might have been. Instead of striking and holding the fish's stomach as it had intended to, it caught the rear portion of the body and severed the tail, taking perhaps a half-inch of the body meat with it.

A frantic jerk permitted the little bass to pull free, but the loss of its tail threw it out of control and it spun and circled helplessly through the water. This was an opportunity that could not be wasted and the large female bass surged to attack. She snatched the smaller bass broadside in her mouth and streaked away from the turtle's area, putting on considerable pressure with her jaws and crushing her prey as she swam.

After a few minutes she slowed, spat out the fish and immediately took it back into her mouth head foremost. It took her a little while but she managed to swallow it. And now, with her hunger appeased, she cruised at a moderate pace back toward her territory beside the sunken boat. She approached it warily, alert for any danger to herself that may have come here during her absence, but there was none. Smoothly she moved into her familiar position beside the hulk in its heaviest shadows and remained there quietly the rest of the night.

III

THE THIRD DAY
OF MAY

EVEN after daylight had come, the female largemouth bass was disinclined to move, and for
many hours she stayed close to the old hulk. Not
until midafternoon was the smaller bass she had
eaten fully digested; as the wind died in late afternoon and the rippled surface of Oak Lake flattened
out to assume its usual mirror calm of evening, once
again she took up the hunt.

She followed the same path she had taken the
evening before when heading for the channel, but this
time she made two brief detours en route. The first
was to inspect briefly the area about the log half-
sunken in the sand and partially out of the water
where she had caught the little bullfrog about thirty
hours ago. A small crayfish was poking about beside

it and she had it in her stomach almost before the little crustacean realized danger was threatening.

Continuing toward the channel, she made her second slight detour just before reaching it, veering closer to shore to where a large ancient willow tree projected out over the lake, its huge roots half in the earth and half in the water. Numerous times before in the nooks and crannies of this root system she had captured crayfish and minnows, and so she would try here again now.

This time, however, the area seemed barren of life at first. Disinclined to give up too quickly, the female bass positioned herself in a dark natural crevice formed by two of the roots and waited. There was always the possibility that some unwary creature would swim within range of her strike. She poised there for many minutes and then there came a faint plip on the surface and two feet above her a pattern of ripples spread out from a rather large floating insect.

Its squat, stubby body was black and there were short bristles about the head portion and a rather long fuzzy tail trailing behind. For a few seconds it just lay quietly on the surface and the bass watched it with increasing interest. Then it twitched delicately and the movement excited her. She left her concealment and began rising toward it, and as she did so the creature made several little darts across the surface toward shore. Lest it escape from her, the bass sped to the attack and the water surface erupted violently as she snatched it.

Instantly she felt a sharp sting in her jaw as the barb of a hook dug deeply into the gristly tissue and stuck there. She leaped high out of the water and shook her head violently, her gill plates spread wide, attempting to dislodge the fishing lure, but it had found a solid rest and held tenaciously.

The bass surged out toward deeper water but was slowed by a tremendous drag against her and within a dozen feet it had succeeded in turning her back toward shore. Now she made an angling run for the tangled willow roots in an attempt to take refuge in the catacombs they afforded, but again the pressure stopped and turned her before she could reach them.

Her strength was fading rapidly; twice more she broke the surface and flapped strenuously in her desperate effort to get free, but she was no match for the skill and power being exerted against her. A few more halfhearted surges were all she could manage and then, exhausted, she turned on her side and felt herself being drawn toward shore. As the water shal-

lowed and the shoreline drew close she made one final
frantic effort to get free, but again she lost.

A hand reached down into the water and a thumb
entered her mouth as fingers closed over her lower
jaw, and she was lifted high out of the water, her tail
flopping feebly in protest.

"Hey, Homer," the angler called, "here's dinner,
by golly!"

A hundred feet or so away a tall man hunkered
beside a small fire over which a blackened coffeepot
was steaming. He nodded, got to his feet and saun-
tered over to his friend, grinning broadly. He inspected the bass and nodded again, approvingly.
"Three pounds," he said, then added, "maybe more.
Nice."

"I had a hunch one might just be laying under
that willow," the angler said, undeniably pleased
with himself. He was a shorter man, well built, and in
the hand opposite that holding the bass he clenched
the handle of a long, limber flyrod. "Got some nice
jumps out of him. Almost had me in the roots once.
Say, what do you make of that?"

He laid his rod on the ground and pointed at the
gash across the back of the bass. His companion
looked more closely, removed the pipe from his mouth
and blew out a cloud of smoke.

"Huh. Looks like he might've been hit by an outboard motor prop. Don't often see that. He's lucky it didn't cut him in half."

The angler agreed. "Won't hurt the meat, I guess. Think this one's enough for tonight?"

His companion shrugged. "Depends on how hungry you are. Me, I could eat most of it myself, way I feel."

The other man laughed. "Me too. I'll try for a couple more." He removed the bass-bug lure from the fish's mouth. "Looks like maybe we're going to have a pretty good weekend."

Taking a chain-link stringer from his bag, he shoved one of the clips through the lower and upper lips of the bass, snapped it closed and dropped it back into the water, attaching the long loose end to a root. The taller man returned to his duties at the campsite and the angler began casting again, shooting the bass-bug expertly ahead of him into the water along the channel. In rapid succession he caught five more bass, three of which were rather small and these he released gently, while the two he kept were each about pound-sized.

Returning to the stringer he laid his rod aside and carried all three fish to a nearby barkless log. In turn he rapped the heads of the fish with the handle of his knife and then filleted them, removing a fine slab of firm white meat from each side. It was expertly done and there was remarkably little waste. The skeletal remains of the three fish — entrails and backbone still connecting head and tail — he pitched into the shallow water a foot from shore and then he washed the six fillets and carried them back to the camp.

And before long the night air was filled with an appetizing aroma of woodsmoke and bass fillets fried to a crisp golden brown.

*　　*　　*

The minnows came first to the remains of the big female bass, just as darkness was falling. They darted nervously about, tearing away little bits of meat or clotted strings of viscera. Often when one of them snatched away a piece too large to swallow at once, he was chased by the others and strenuous little tugs-of-war resulted.

Insects came too — water insects drawn by the scent of the blood and airborne insects drawn by the aroma of that portion of the remains not entirely covered by the very shallow water.

Though it was quite late in the evening for them to still be flying, four yellowjacket hornets alighted upon the exposed portion and began feeding greedily, oblivious of the activity below the water's surface.

A giant water bug — water tiger, as it is sometimes called — fully three inches long skimmed up from the deeper waters directly to a meaty portion of the large bass and sank its beak into it and began at once to suck out the juices. A fierce insect that flies or swims with equal agility, its presence here frightened the minnows away. A giant water bug was wholly capable of chasing, catching and killing a minnow. It was not, in fact, afraid to attack fish four times its own size, and quite frequently it preyed upon other insects or occasionally even attacked small frogs.

The big insect gorged itself quickly and swam sluggishly to shore, where it crawled beneath a piece of bark to rest. At once the minnows returned and, now that it was full dark, the crayfish came too, attracted as the others were by the scent trails wafting through the water. Soon there were a half-dozen of them crawling over the carcasses, pulling at them, attempting to drag them to the safety of deeper waters.

And little by little as the night progressed, the last remains of the female largemouth bass were disappearing.

IV

THE FOURTH DAY
OF MAY

B Y shortly after midnight, when the nearby camp-
fire had become a bed of dim embers, most of
the bass entrails had been devoured, principally by
crayfish. The two smaller fish carcasses were gone,
each having been dragged away by immature snapping turtles. As always, there would be no waste in
nature. Even now the larger crayfish were continuing to feed on the greatly diminished remains of the
large female bass when a sudden disturbance in the
water to one side caused them to shoot away into
deeper water to seek hiding places.

Cause of the disturbance was a large year-old male
raccoon wading in the shallows seeking frogs or crayfish or any other edibles. He, too, had now caught
scent of the remains and he sloshed carelessly toward

the spot, heedless of the noise he made. For a time he inspected what was left, turning the residue over with his handlike front paws. There was precious little left to eat of the body meat or entrails, but a fair amount of flesh still clung to the head. With a peculiar daintiness, the raccoon dipped his snout below the water and picked up the head in his teeth, braced his feet against the bare backbone and jerked it free. Jauntily he carried the fish head off into the woods.

Though large for his age, this raccoon was by no means as large as he would one day be. Including his ten-inch ringed tail, he was just under three feet long and weighed fourteen pounds. In another year or two he would measure forty inches or more and perhaps weigh in excess of twenty-five pounds. Nevertheless, he was large for his age.

If matters had turned out differently, he would probably now be carrying this morsel to his den as food for a litter of his young. But about a month ago, just before his mate was due to deliver, she had been struck by an auto and killed and so now he was on his own and would very likely remain that way until next February, when he would seek another mate.

He carried the head to the nearby hollow tree in which he now made his lair and there, at the base of it, gnawed contentedly until the flesh was all gone and only the bony superstructure remained. And then, because he still had a measure of the playfulness of a cub in him, he batted the head back and forth in the clearing, sometimes tossing it into the air and catching it and at other times thrusting it from him and then tearing after it, catching it while it was still bumping along the ground, grappling with it and then rolling over and over while growling fiercely.

At length he grew weary of his game and carried the remains a short distance into the woods, where he dropped it and continued toward the lake. He emerged on the shore quite near to where he had found the fish, and this time he entered the water stealthily.

He waded slowly through water four or five inches deep, feeling with dextrous front paws under rocks and weed piles. Without any great difficulty he caught two small crayfish, which he crunched greedily between sharp white teeth. A moment later he had hold of a large bullfrog tadpole but it wriggled out of his grasp an instant after he caught it.

He sniffed about curiously for a little while along the shore and then his nose led him to the log where the fish had been filleted. In the grass here he found a

chunk of the liver of one of the fish and he wolfed it
down. For a long while after that he stared at the
little campsite and then approached it slowly.

The two men were stretched out in sleeping bags
on either side of the almost dead fire, and the raccoon
showed no indication of fear as he ambled up to them.
He sniffed at the foot of one bag and then crossed to
the other and walked deliberately between the embers
and the sleeping man, as if reveling in his boldness
and daring.

A few feet away from them he found a canvas pack
on which the straps had not been refastened and with
a bit of fumbling he managed to open the flap and
begin rummaging. He showed no interest in a plastic
container filled with fishing lures nor in a tightly
rolled-up rain slicker. But when he found a white
paper sack filled with hard candies, he ripped it
apart, strewing them in all directions. He bit one of
them in half but appeared not to like it and spat it
out, then turned his attention to a small can of lard.
It took a little while for him to figure out what to do,
but finally he managed to pry open the hinged lid
with his teeth while holding the sides of the can with
his front feet. He sniffed gingerly at the white material and then stuck his front paws into it in turn,
each paw scooping out a heavy gob. He licked it

tentatively, decided he didn't like that, either, and began rubbing it off on the ground.

"Hey! Get out of there!"

A beam of light speared the darkness and the startled raccoon jumped and spun around. The taller of the two men was sitting upright, reaching for a shoe which his flashlight beam had locked on. The other man was stirring.

Curiously unafraid, the raccoon loped off and entered the woods again on the opposite side of the camp, not even bothered when the shoe thumped to the ground to one side of him. Behind him the irritation in the voices dissolved into chuckles and then became laughter.

He traveled a fairly direct course now, heading straight for the barnyard of a half-mile-distant farm which fronted in part on Oak Lake. But as he approached it he became more cautious. There were dogs here, he knew — dogs that were only too eager for an opportunity to nab such an interloper as he.

With frequent stops to listen carefully, he made his way to the barn and entered it. In one of the stalls a horse saw him and snorted and then stamped its foot, and in another a pair of twin Holstein calves scrambled to the far side and hugged the wall as he ambled past, but they made no outcry.

In the tack room he climbed onto a bench and poked about in a variety of containers, spilling nuts and rivets, bolts, leather straps and other hardware materials to the floor, and now for the first time one of the dogs barked uncertainly.

He didn't pay any attention to it and continued his rummaging. From the tack room he passed into the milking room and amused himself by jumping through rows of stanchions. From there he entered the smaller separating room, where shiny milk cans were stacked upside down and a large cream separator and churn dominated one wall. The smells here intrigued him and he scrambled atop the separator. Its stainless steel trappings were smooth and clean and so he directed his attention to the churn. There was a small open door near the top and to get there he attempted a flying leap to the top of the milk can pile. He landed where he had intended but the inverted cans were precariously stacked and with a tremendous clatter the whole business tumbled, with him in the middle of it all.

Though shaken up he wasn't injured, but the noise frightened him badly and so did the savage barking which came immediately after. At once he plunged for the doorway, which appeared open. It was screened, and he struck the screening a tremendous blow, ripping it. Slightly dazed, he squirmed through the hole he had made, ripping it wider in his passage, and then he was in the barnyard and running at full tilt toward the adjoining marsh.

The dogs were not far behind, and as he shot a quick glance over his shoulder he saw the lights in farmhouse and barn flare into life. Both dogs were whining and growling as they ran, and suddenly a deeper fear bloomed in the raccoon as he realized how very close to him they were, and he put every ounce of his strength into outdistancing them.

The dogs continued to close the gap between them, but now the soil had become spongy and he was entering the marsh area. Heedless of the racket he made, he thrashed through the dried cattails and spattered through deeper pockets of water which he knew would help hide his scent. Before long he was swimming more than running, and now he slowed and proceeded more quietly.

The dogs were barking again as they splashed through the swampy shallows, their cries filled with frustration at having lost the raccoon's trail. Satisfied, he continued his measured progress and the barks grew fainter with the distance.

The raccoon traversed nearly the whole of the marsh before finally stopping on the small low island upon which a single dead tree stood, its naked arms stretching upward to greet the breaking dawn. Shaking himself to rid his fur of water and mud, the raccoon now felt a weariness overtaking him. He had had a busy night.

With the assurance of one who had been here before — which indeed he had — the raccoon ambled over to the tree and ducked into a small opening at its base. Inside it opened up to a moderate-sized den with a bed of dry leaves and grasses, and here he curled up and immediately fell asleep.

*   *   *

It was late afternoon when he awakened and the reeds and lily pads were bejeweled with tiny crystal beads of the light rain that had fallen while he slept. He squirmed out of the opening and walked to the water's edge, where there was a flurry of activity as a score of small frogs leaped away in alarm. He stood there quietly for a time and in a few moments his gaze fastened upon the slight lifting of a bit of vegetation close to shore. He pounced upon it, grabbing and clinging with his front feet and biting rapidly through the debris. There was a brief struggle and then he let go with his mouth, and his forepaws uncovered the carcass of the small bullfrog he had just slain. He chewed it up methodically and the small bones crackled beneath his bite.

Before he had finished with it, however, a movement above him caught his attention. Other wildlife had seen it, too, and the chorus of trills from myriad red-winged blackbirds and occasional grunts and croaks from frogs were abruptly stilled as a large brown bird came gliding low over the reeds, its flashing white rump patch identifying it as a marsh hawk. Almost at the same moment another approached from the opposite direction. Since these birds of prey posed no real threat to him, the raccoon watched them with some interest.

As the birds neared one another they began a slow, graceful circling and gained altitude gradually, all the while crying and whistling softly to one another. In a little while they were hardly more than specks against a now cloudless sky, still circling but about one hundred yards apart.

As if by command, both birds suddenly closed their wings and dropped. Down and down they plummeted until it seemed they couldn't possibly save themselves from smashing into the marsh, with devastating results to themselves. With only inches to spare and traveling at fantastic speed, their wings spread simultaneously and they shot toward one an-

other, a pair of brown blurs. Their leading wing
edges racketed through the tops of withered reed
blades and occasionally struck a dry cattail left from
last fall, causing it to explode in a great burst of
fluffy white cottonlike down.

Collision between the two birds seemed unavoidable
when both angled sharply upward, still heading toward one another. They met a dozen yards over the
marsh and clung together as if they were feathered
magnets, the wings of the female opening to embrace
the male. Their momentum carried them upward still
another twenty feet or more in oblivious rapture.
Entwined in a brown ball, they fell together, and
broke apart only when a few feet above the reeds.
The female soared gracefully to the dead tree on the
raccoon's island and settled there high on a springy
branch and commenced preening herself, but the
male went wild.

Up he flew and higher yet and then down in a
screaming dive to smash his way through yards of
dry reeds, the whole episode punctuated by the white
bursts of fuzz as old cattails were struck. Again he
beat his way skyward in erratic flight interrupted by
breathtaking loops and rolls. High he flew, higher
than before, and then abruptly deflated and tumbled
crazily, wings flopping disjointedly, as if all the life

had departed from him. Close to the marsh he caught himself once more and climbed again.

But now the female marsh hawk catapulted away from her perch and skimmed elegantly toward the southwestern edge of the marsh, and her adoring swain, continuing his acrobatics, followed on high.

By this time the raccoon had lost interest. He left the island and headed back through the marsh toward his den tree in the woods. In transit he caught and devoured four more frogs and so it was early evening when he reached the firm ground just a few hundred yards from the barnyard. Heavy clouds were building up on the western horizon and a storm was evidently in prospect.

He proceeded cautiously now, sticking to cover and giving the barnyard a wide berth, the memory of the two dogs chasing him still fresh enough to bother him. He followed the edge of a field of winter wheat already taller than he. It masked his progress, and he was nearly to the woods when a large insect buzzed noisily past his head, turned and buzzed past again, even closer.

Instinctively the raccoon shied, taking it at first for a bumblebee, but then becoming very nearly panic-stricken when the insect buzzed past his head a third time, even closer, and he got a better look at it.

61

He turned and ran, dodging this way and that, attempting to hide his head or slap away the insect, but it followed him persistently.

This was a robust bot fly, a heavy, swift-flying bee-like insect which was now highly intent upon laying an egg or two on the raccoon where they would be most likely to survive: which meant in the nostrils, on his lip or on the fur at the wrists of his forepaws.

She was accustomed to the frantic exertions of mammals such as this raccoon to get away and knew all the tricks of breaking their defenses. She employed them now. She paced the raccoon, biding her time, and when he briefly raised his head to look for her she arrowed in with great speed and unerring accuracy. She touched his lip just below the nose and in that instant deposited an egg there. The raccoon tumbled over in a frenzied roll but as soon as he regained his feet she drove in again and this time another egg was attached to the wrist fur of his right forepaw.

The raccoon galloped into the underbrush fringing the field and ran pell-mell into the woods, but he was no longer being pursued. Satisfied with herself, the bot fly had withdrawn and was now buzzing lazily toward the barnyard.

She alighted on a fence post a short distance from

the barn and commenced cleaning her legs, wings and antennae — a procedure followed each time she had finished exerting herself to lay eggs upon some mammal, as she just had on the raccoon. The maneuvering necessary in such a function was very tiring, and so now, after cleaning herself, she inspected the top of the fence post and found a hole just larger than her body which angled downward into the wood and which seemed an ideal place for her to rest free from the watchful eyes of predators.

As she crawled into the hole a sharp gust of wind tugged at her hindquarters, but she pulled herself into the dark interior and followed the little passageway downward until it came to an abrupt dead end three inches from the opening. And here she became still and slept.

V

THE FIFTH DAY
OF MAY

THERE was little doubt that those two eggs the
bot fly had laid upon the raccoon would hatch.
The one deposited on the animal's wrist fur would
probably take somewhat longer, for it would not be
stimulated until the next time he cleaned himself. As
he licked the fur on his feet and legs the egg would
dislodge onto his tongue and be withdrawn into his
mouth and hatch there very quickly.

As for the egg deposited on his lip, chances were
that it had hatched within mere minutes of being laid
there. The female bot fly herself had been deposited as
an egg similarly on the lip of a fat woodchuck last
year about this time. The instant a bit of moisture
had touched that egg, the fragile shell had disinte-
grated and she had emerged as a tiny larva almost

64

too small to be seen. Instinctively she had squirmed toward the wet warmth of the inner mouth. It had only taken a few minutes to reach the saliva, and subsequently she had been swallowed.

She had had no eyes then so the interior darkness of the animal had not concerned her. The juices of the stomach stimulated her immediately and she clung tenaciously to the stomach wall and began to burrow. It had taken many strenuous hours of alternately burrowing and resting to make her way through the infinitesimal hole she chewed in the stomach lining, and she merely relaxed and floated free in the body cavity for a long time afterward, absorbing new energy from the very juices in which she floated.

At last she had begun her long journey to the surface, forcing her way into muscle fibers and fatty tissues, stopping often to feed and leaving behind a little trail of partially destroyed and slightly inflamed tissue. For the most part she did not stay to feed in one place long enough to do any really serious harm to her host, but it would be some time before the woodchuck's system could repair the scattered minor damages she was causing.

Of this she knew nothing. Her only concern was to gorge almost continuously on the tissues through which she slowly moved. Now and again she paused for long periods to feed in one spot deep in the muscle fibers and here, each time, a small cyst would develop as the host animal's body attempted to protect itself.

It took many weeks for the larva to eat its way to the subcutaneous membranes below the woodchuck's fur and outer skin, and here she paused a final time to feed in earnest. The point of her emergence was just in front of the woodchuck's left hip and only an inch or so from the spine. This was among the least disturbed areas during the mammal's daily cleansing operations, for it was one of the hardest areas for the animal to reach.

The female bot fly larva fed and grew here for quite a long time. The days became weeks and the weeks stretched into months. When she had first reached this area just under the skin of the woodchuck she was scarcely a quarter-inch long and less than a third that in diameter, but as summer dwindled into autumn and then the winter winds began to howl, she grew remarkably. By late February she was as large as she would get in her larval state and she was a decidedly ugly creature. She was now a segmented maggot an inch and a half in length and over a half-inch thick. She was an unappealing dingy gray in color and her body was essentially formless except for her head, which had grown large, sightless eyes. The strange, rasplike mouthparts, with which she could continue to shred the muscle tissue so that the fluids could more readily break them down for her to swallow and digest, had enlarged greatly and were daily causing discomfort and damage to her host.

The increase in her size had, of course, made quite a large lump to form on the back of the woodchuck. This lump was known as a warble; and, because of its habit of forming such lumps on various kinds of mammals, including cattle and sheep, farmers commonly called her species a warble fly, and they hated her with a passion. A single adult bot fly buzzing over a herd of cattle or horses could cause them to stampede in panic.

Instinctively knowing that the time was drawing close for her final metamorphosis, the larva had at last turned her attention away from the muscle fibers of the woodchuck and set about gnawing a hole about the diameter of a pencil through the animal's outer skin.

February became March and then March began to wane before the larva finally thrust her way out of the opening she had made in the skin and fell to the ground while the woodchuck was dining on some freshly sprouted clover near the mouth of its burrow. Immediately upon hitting the ground, the larva dug a hole just large enough for her body and buried herself to a depth of six inches.

And here, underground, the ugly gray skin of the maggot split and fell away, revealing a dark purplish-brown pupa, upon the tough shell of which could be seen only vaguely the outlines of the adult bot fly. For three weeks the pupa had remained underground here in a dormant state and then, as the late April sun had warmed the earth, the final transition had taken place. The pupal case split and from within it emerged the adult female bot fly that was herself. She had forced her way to the surface and sat there quietly for many long minutes, allowing her damp, furled wings to open and dry into the stiff strong membranes they were now.

Within days of her emergence she had met and mated with a newly emerged male bot fly, and within her body now were over six hundred fertile eggs waiting to be deposited. Since then she had been very busy. Last evening's raccoon was the seventh mammal upon which her eggs had been laid: sometimes only one egg, but occasionally as many as four or five when her aim had been a little off and there was a chance the eggs would not reach the moisture of the mouth.

As soon as daylight came again, she would leave

this fence-post burrow and search for other mammals upon which to lay still more eggs. She drew her legs up tightly against her body as if in reaction to the keening whine of wind hissing past her hole entrance. Actually, the blowing of this wind, which had begun about midnight, did not bother her as much as the heavy rumbling of approaching thunder. The deep booming sound had begun several hours before dawn, causing the fence post to vibrate, and she stirred uneasily.

At one point the rumbling and vibration bothered her so that she backed out of the hole, holding tightly so the strong wind would not rip her away. She hesitated at the mouth of the hole, her front feet still inside the cavity. Abruptly a huge drop of rain smacked into her body, nearly loosing her grip, and in a moment more drops were hitting the post with audible splats. On wing she could best the wind if necessary, but she could not fly through pelting rain, and so she continued to clutch the burrow entrance tightly and crouch there as if contemplating what next to do.

With a fury the clouds broke and a deluge of rain lashed down. The hissing drops beat her unmercifully and she was left with no alternative. It was with the greatest of difficulty that she was able to drag herself back into the hole and crawl inward until her body was just below the level of the top of the post. Had the storm been no more than a brief thunder-shower the hole would have protected her, but throughout the rest of the night the heavy rain fell steadily while brilliant forks of blue-white lightning ripped jagged streaks across the sky and sharp cracks of thunder vibrated the earth.

The storm ended with the dawning, and by the time the sun arose the sky was clear and the air sweet and fresh from the drenching it had undergone. The trees and fields were alive with birds rejoicing in the new day. From out in the marsh the red-winged blackbirds warbled incessantly, and robins and blue-birds, fox sparrows and meadowlarks sang from trees and fence rows and fields.

The female bot fly was still alive, but just barely. The hole into which she had crept had become trap rather than haven. It had filled to the brim with water and she had almost drowned. Slowly, dazedly, she backed out of the hole and weakly positioned herself in the bright sunlight. Until her wings dried and she warmed thoroughly she would be unable to fly, and so she was very vulnerable.

Too vulnerable.

A meadowlark perched on a telephone line some

forty yards away saw the slight movement she made backing out of the hole and immediately fluttered down to the post. Almost before its feet had found a purchase, the bird snapped up the insect, crushed her in its sharp bill, and swallowed her.

And so the career of this bot fly ended as it had begun — in the stomach of another creature.

*   *   *

After swallowing the large insect the meadowlark fluffed its feathers and continued to sit on the fence post for a considerable while. Every now and then he raised his head and a melodious song swept out of his throat and filled the morning air with the pleasantness and brightness of the sun.

He was a strikingly handsome bird, three years old and in the prime of his development. True, his upper feathers of back and neck were a rather pale buff color shading into darker ruddy brown, but here any degree of drabness ended. Three stripes of brilliant yellow plumage began at the base of his beak: one which swept back over the top of his crown to the back of his neck and two which passed above the eye on either side and nearly merged with the center one toward the rear of the bird's head.

But what was most immediately obvious and striking about his appearance was his breast. The feathering here was a startling lemon yellow, unbroken except for a broad crescent of jet black which crossed the front of him as if it were a sash of ebony. The horns of this crescent projected upward on each side to the cheek, where they terminated in a larger patch of black.

The bird's alert eye was a rich cinnamon red and it missed little of what happened around him, just as at this moment he spied in the deep grass beside the farm lane a wolf spider that had run into a saucer-sized clearing and stood there with its two front legs upraised as it tested the air for prey. The tables were turned as it became prey itself; the meadowlark swooped downward in a smooth glide and snatched it up.

The handsome bird swallowed the spider and then crouched in the grass for a moment as if deciding upon his next move. It was not long in coming. Boldly he waddled through several feet of deeper grasses and stepped out onto the rutted wagon path. As if he had an important engagement to keep, he determinedly marched down the road away from the barnyard.

Unlike by far the greater majority of perching birds, he neither hopped nor ran. Instead, he walked quite smoothly, as a chicken does, placing one foot in front of the other in a very methodical manner. He kept turning his head slightly to one side, scanning the open space ahead of him, and before he walked over thirty feet he had caught and eaten a small dark brown beetle. He continued his walk and in the next fifteen minutes devoured a stinkbug, a ladybird beetle and a black-and-white speckled moth nearly as large as the bot fly had been.

From far behind him a rumbling noise caught his attention, and he stood erect and saw coming toward him from the barnyard a tractor driven by a youth of about fourteen. The bird squatted where he was and waited until the tractor was almost upon him, and then he leaped high into the air and sped away in a wide arc with his characteristically peculiar fluttering flight.

The arc of his trajectory carried him back toward the electric wires upon which he had been sitting when first he spied the bot fly, but this time he aimed for the top of the pole instead. He fluttered in that same rather heavy fashion until he was above the pole and then set his wings and glided until just an instant before he reached it. Immediately upon landing on the circular post-top, he flicked his tail several times in succession, displaying the startling white feathers that rimmed his tail — a curious little action he performed almost every time he landed.

As the wagon passed beneath him he threw back his head and once again the sweet notes warbled from his throat and carried far in the still morning air. Even over the noisy clatter of the motor, the lad on the tractor heard the cheerful song and he raised his eyes to look at the bird and grinned.

Not at all alarmed and, in fact, rather curious, the meadowlark watched the wagon continue down the lane past another two poles and then maneuver a bit in order to back up to a small two-wheeled wagon lying upside down in a little pull-off area. Cutting the ignition, the youth leaped down, righted the wagon with something of an effort and then laughed delightedly as a large cottontail rabbit leaped up and bobbed away, its tail flashing as it hopped through the tall weeds and dried buffalo grass. When the rabbit had disappeared from sight he attached the wagon tongue to the tractor hitch, climbed back to his seat and drove off again toward the barnyard.

All this activity the meadowlark had watched with interest but he did not pay much attention to the disappearing wagon. He was more intrigued by the rectangle of stunted sickly yellow grass beneath where the wagon had been resting. Little moisture or sunlight had found its way through the cracks of the small wagon bed and the ground there was hard and dry.

The meadowlark sprang from his perch and fluttered to the spot, and his white tail feathers, mostly hidden while he perched, were again plainly visible in flight. He landed lightly, characteristically flicked his tail again a time or two, then set about exploring the previously hidden patch of ground.

The protective covering afforded by the wagon bed had provided a haven for a variety of insects, and very easily he caught and devoured several crickets and spiders, a couple of beetles and a caterpillar. On the ground here there was a scattering of wheat grains that had apparently fallen there when the wagon was overturned, but for the moment the bird paid no attention to them. The insects demanded priority concern. They were his principal bill of fare, and though he was not opposed to eating seeds, and very often did, the insects always took precedence if there was a choice. Later in the summer, when the weeds and grasses of the fields fruited, his diet would include considerably more seeds, but at this time of the year they were usually scarce and not really worth the effort of seeking out.

Not until he had finished feasting on what insects

had been available here did he turn his attention to the wheat kernels and spend a quarter-hour recovering all he could find. At the end of this time his crop was tightly packed and bulging beneath his upper breast feathers as if he had swallowed a golf ball.

He took to wing once again and this time he flew to the fringe of trees which separated the prairie from Oak Lake. Alighting on the sandy shore he walked to the water, drank deeply and then fluttered to the very peak of the tallest tree overlooking the prairie and his singing before was as nothing compared to the enthusiastic burst of melody which throbbed from his throat now. Over and again he repeated his clear ringing song and the sound of it carried remarkably far over the fields and into the woods and even a great distance over the waters of the lake.

The two anglers who were bass fishing along the channel heard the call and cocked their heads toward it. The taller of the pair nodded and pointed his pipestem toward the trees. "It's really spring when you hear the larks calling like that," he commented. "He's probably trying to stir up a lady love."

The comment was accurate. In the opposite direction from the big tree, beyond the prairie and lane, across the wheat field which adjoined it and into another prairie beyond that, a female meadow-lark was similarly cocking her head and listening to the notes rolling through the air toward her.

She was not quite as large as the male bird and, while her coloration was approximately the same, it was not as brilliant as his. Her wingspan of nine inches was almost two inches less than his and her bill was somewhat thicker and not as sharply tapered to its point.

She paused, listening intently, for five minutes or more and then, as if reaching a decision, sprang into the air with that same sort of fluttering flight that he had exhibited and sailed over the fields toward his perch. Fifty feet or so from the big tree she glided down and settled in an area of matted-down grasses. Without hesitation the male — who had seen her coming only instants after she took off — jumped from his perch and flew down to join her.

He landed two or three feet distant from her, flicked his tail a few times more than usual and then stood up to his full height, lifted his head until the beak was pointing straight up, and again sang his love song. Four times in succession he sang it and the female lifted her head in the same manner, but she remained mute.

Now the male, continuing to hold his head high,

commenced strutting pompously about, circling her time and again, stopping only occasionally to sing his song. At times his wings drooped very low, actually trailing on the ground, and at other times his tail feathers lifted high and he marched about with his wings slightly outstretched.

At last the female, seemingly satisfied with what she saw and heard, crouched low and dropped her head until her lower bill and neck were resting on the ground. The male fluttered to her and the mating was accomplished swiftly and without further exhibition. In another minute he took to the air and resumed his perch atop the high tree, and now his song as it rolled forth was subtly different: in a manner triumphant, yet challenging at the same time. In giving voice to it he was establishing territorial rights, laying claim to the several hundred feet of area surrounding the female still on the ground.

For her own part, the female lost no time in setting about building her nest, and though the male did not assist her in the actual construction, he did keep a sharp lookout from above over this area they had claimed as their own. If any other meadowlarks entered it, he would dart from his high perch and clash vigorously with them until he had driven them off.

The nest would be intricately built of grasses
woven skillfully together, coarse on the outside and
hard to distinguish from the grass surrounding it,
yet lined with soft smooth fibers inside and completely domed over so that the eggs, when laid, would
be shielded from marauding eyes. When the nest was
finished there would be one final phase of construction: a tiny path would be made stretching three or
four feet through the grass and leading directly to
the arched opening of the nest. It would originate at
a small clearing nearby. In this manner it would not
be necessary for the birds to betray the location of
the nest by landing directly beside it.

Within a few days after the nest was finished the
female would lay her four, five or six brilliant white
eggs speckled thinly with chestnut brown. They
would hatch in just over a week. Only then would the
male return to his mate's side, to help her in the
feeding and raising of their family. But for now he
would merely guard this territory against intruders.

With the coming of evening the female flew off a
little distance and fed, stopped briefly at the lakeshore to drink and then returned to spend the night
in her partially constructed nest. As soon as she had
come back, the male flew off on his own, flitting about
in short hopping flights through the meadow as he

caught a variety of insects, predominantly crickets and quite a good number of wolf spiders.

His hunger satisfied at last, and with heavy rain-clouds building up again in the west as the darkness was closing in rapidly, he made a quick flight to the lake, drank deeply and then headed back toward a spot where he would settle to sleep in the deep grass not very far from where his mate was roosting.

But as he took off from the water's edge, he spurted a stream of viscous material from his vent, the residue of the day's digested, partially digested or undigested food matter. This material fell to the earth beside a rotting log which had made the soil spongy. And within the meadowlark's waste were several undigested grains of wheat from the number he had picked up early in the day where the farm wagon had lain.

A half hour later the storm broke, and it was another night of gusty winds and slashing rains.

VI

THE SIXTH DAY
OF MAY

IT was in the predawn darkness that one of the
undigested wheat kernels the meadowlark had ex-
pelled was washed into a small crevice in the loamy
earth. An inch and a half beneath the surface it
lodged firmly. But while the rain moved the other
two undigested kernels about, they remained on the
surface.

Once again, as had become customary lately, the
rain ceased at dawn, although a heavy bank of clouds
continued to move slowly over the area. It was perhaps an hour after daybreak when a pair of mourn-
ing doves alighted on the lakeshore close by and
waddled across the narrow strip of hard-packed sand
to the water's edge. Since neither would drink again
until evening, both of them now drank at length.

They were apparently in no hurry to move on and inspected the surrounding area in a rather desultory fashion. Every now and then one or another of the streamlined pair would stop to pick up and swallow some select pieces of grit to aid in the grinding up of the food to be eaten during this day.

The ambling of one of the birds, a handsome male with large soft eyes, took it farther up the shore to where the sand gave way to soil. He was still several feet distant from the rotting log when he spied the pair of freshly rain-washed wheat grains. He waddled to them at once and ate them, not knowing or caring that they had been eaten once already by another bird. Then he continued his meandering explorations.

For the better part of half an hour the two birds stayed in the same area, but the single wheat kernel that had been washed into the crevice remained undetected, even though from directly above that crack it could still be seen. This condition did not last long.

Shortly after the departure of the birds on wings that whistled clearly when they took off, it began to rain again, and since the earth was already well saturated from the night's downpour, there was a good bit of run-off over the surface. The little crevice filled with water and the earth rimming its sides became weakened and suddenly collapsed and buried the grain.

Off and on during the remainder of the day the rains fell, but not again as heavily as during the night. And by evening a considerable change had taken place in the grain of wheat. Its rough outer husk, considerably softened to begin with by its journey through the alimentary tract of the meadowlark, had now begun to deteriorate. The moisture it had been holding back had become too much, and the husk absorbed it until it could absorb no more and then the moisture began seeping through to bathe the kernel itself.

A faint crack appeared and widened between the two halves of the kernel, and the moisture entered this and soaked the nucleus — a tiny grainlike oblong connecting the two kernel halves at one end. And in the darkness here beneath the ground a spark of life was kindled in that nucleus; it began to swell slightly and there was a minute but increasing movement of cells as germination commenced.

VII

THE ELEVENTH DAY
OF MAY

C ONDITIONS for the sprouting of seeds could not
have been much more ideal than they were during the four days that followed. Intermittent rains
fell gently, and during those periods that the clouds
broke, the sun shone down warmly and created a
veritable hothouse condition on the earth's surface.

Forty-eight hours after the initial flicker of life
became evident within the wheat kernel nucleus, the
first tiny nodule of root began protruding from it
and, once begun, grew swiftly. By the middle of the
night it had pushed itself out beyond the end of the
kernel and turned downward. Within hours three
other milk-white rootlets were following it.

With surprising speed, now that movement was begun, the four small roots radiated outward beneath
the kernel, pushing through the softened earth and

going around, over or under small pebbles or the hard woody roots of trees or shrubs that were encountered. They anchored themselves securely as they spread throughout the third day, and when they had become an inch or more in length they sprouted even smaller hairlike fibers to better grip the earth and seek out its moisture.

By the fourth morning it was the seed itself which moved. It had been wedged in the crevice parallel to the ground surface, but now it pivoted on its rooted end and raised itself until the tip was almost straight up, and then the kernel began moving toward the surface, raised on a strong pillar of stem.

As the seed moved upward, the crack between the two kernel halves widened even more, and when it was a half-inch from ground level a new, pale yellowish-green spear of growth began projecting from the upper end.

And then yesterday morning, just below the surface, the kernel had broken apart and remained where it was, while the upper spear of new growth shoved aside a small clod of dirt and poked itself into the air. The sun was shining and the wheat spear drank up the life-giving rays. Within its cells the process of producing chlorophyll began, and in a very short time the sprout had grown deeper in color and was a bright emerald green.

Growth of the seedling was comparatively slow during the day, but that night it speeded up. The spear pushed itself up to a height of nearly an inch, and the lateral buds which had formed near its tip thrust another spear of growth a half-inch higher. There was another lateral bud at the end of this newer sprout, and so the growth process continued without pause throughout the night and all of today until, by quite late this afternoon, the shoot was fully three inches high and a pair of bright fresh blades were angling out from it.

But the seedling was destined to grow no more.

A faint rustling sound came from the brush to one side and then a large female cottontail rabbit cautiously poked just her head through a screen of weeds. Her nose twitched delicately and rapidly as she tested the air for possible danger and her ears — one of them rather badly tattered — turned this way and that to detect the same. When she had become satisfied that no enemy was present, she emerged entirely from the weedy cover and started across the little clearing with a smooth hopping gait.

It appeared that she would continue without pause to the other side, but just as she came even with the young wheat spike and it was only a foot to her left, she saw it and her nose quivered again. Two more small hops took her to the seedling and she touched her nose to it gently and found it to be fresh and tender and obviously delectable.

She tilted her head a bit and leaned close to the ground and her sharp incisor teeth neatly snipped off the sprout at its base. For a long comical moment she sat utterly still with the stalk sticking from her mouth, much in the manner in which a farmer chews on a long stem of straw. Then she began to eat it. Quickly the shoot was drawn inward as she chewed, disappearing smoothly into her mouth as if of its own volition until only the tiniest tip of green blade remained exposed.

And then even that was gone.

*   *   *

This was the female rabbit's fourth season and she was a wise old doe, highly experienced in the ways of avoiding danger or in escaping from it if it was unexpectedly thrust upon her. Very few of her species survived for over two years the multitude of perils that existed almost perpetually on all sides, and fewer still lived to see three summers. Those that reached her age were a rarity for, along with the

meadow mouse — a tiny rodent which greatly out-
numbered her species — she was one of the most
preyed-upon creatures in this range.

Practically every carnivorous mammal in the area
hunted her kind incessantly, and even the air about
her was not always safe, for out of it hurtled the
numerous deadly hawks or occasional eagles, the
noisy crows and the night-flying owls, which considered fresh rabbit meat a great delicacy.

As a result she was perpetually wary, freezing in
position a hundred times or more each day as her ears
or nose or eyes detected some faint whisper or scent
or slight movement that might betoken peril; and
just as frequently ready to burst into that frantic,
erratic run which was her principal defense.

Within her range, which covered the fields and
woods along much of the southwestern perimeter of
Oak Lake, she knew the precise location of every
woodchuck burrow, hollow log, brush pile or other
hiding place to which she might streak in time of
pursuit. And if the enemy were one who could follow
her into such places — a weasel or snake, for in-
stance — she knew other means of escape: the tiny
spring branch which coursed through the meadow
and woods was always an effective eraser of scent,
and the deep canelike buffalo grass not far from the

highway, through which ran a series of rabbit trails crossing and crisscrossing one another, created a maze hopeless to virtually any pursuer.

Close calls she had undergone by the score, but she had escaped each time and become wiser through their occurrence. One time a fox had actually had his teeth upon her but she had wriggled free at the expense of a shredded ear. Another time a long-eared owl had grabbed her and only the fact that one of her flailing feet luckily struck the bird's stomach and very nearly disemboweled it enabled her to escape. Twice the painful fire of buckshot had stung her, but never mortally, and once she had been forced as a last resort to leap into the lake and swim across a little cove to the opposite side in a final desperate measure to elude a feral house cat. And though other escapes had been as narrow, still she survived.

Now, having finished dining upon the succulent wheat seedling, she resumed her travel, heading southward through the darkening woods that rimmed the lake. Ahead of her a quarter-mile, not far from where the narrow strip of macadam secondary highway passed, was her nest, in which four tiny offspring — fawns, as they were known — awaited her return. These fawns were only eleven days old.

This was by no means her first litter. Far from it,

in fact. In her first summer, following the spring she was born, she had given birth to a litter of four. During her second year she had had three litters, one of five young and two of seven; and last summer she had given birth to three more litters, one of six fawns and two of five. The four in this spring's first litter brought her total offspring to forty-three and, if she continued successfully eluding danger, chances are she would have at least that many more.

Within her breast there beat a passionate mother-love no shallower for these four fawns than for her previous thirty-nine. True, it was a love and protectiveness that would disappear quickly, perhaps in as little time as three or four or five days from now when they became more self-sufficient and scattered away on their own. But for now, and during the whole of their fifteen or sixteen days under her care, they were the most important thing of all in her existence — more important, even, than life was to her.

As she made her way now toward that little, well-hidden nest, she moved along in a rather peculiar manner. Rarely did she ever maintain a steady pace for any length of time. Across small clearings or glades she would move quickly, but she would stop close to the far side and pause rigidly, all senses intently alert. When fully satisfied that nothing dangerous had observed her passage, she would continue another twenty or thirty feet and repeat the process, always staying as close to good cover as possible and taking advantage of anything that happened to be available in which to camouflage herself. It was remarkable how, even in an area of short sparse grass, she could crouch low to the ground and virtually disappear from sight. With her ears laid flat against her neck and back, the only part of her that was clearly visible was her eye. And there were few enemies who could detect only that bright eye, whether in thick cover or sparse grass.

One of her principal defenses — a mechanism upon which she relied heavily for survival and which, in fact, had many times saved her life — was her vision. Although it was not especially keen over very long distances, it was extremely sharp at short range. Her eyes were rather protuberant, and when she crouched low with her ears held flat to her back, her peripheral vision was astounding. Because her eyes were located on the sides of her head rather than to the front, she could see not only frontwards and to both sides, but so far in back of her that only a small wedge of space directly behind her — no more than ten or twelve degrees of the three hundred sixty degrees surrounding her — remained a blind spot.

With such vision as this, there was little likelihood that any enemy could slip up on her undetected.

If an intruder did come along, it was invariably she who saw him first rather than vice versa, and her muscles would bunch beneath her. If whatever it was came too close, then with startling abruptness she would dart out and away, always with a route of escape already all mapped out in her mind; and such route was dependent upon the type of predator it was. If bird of prey, she would quickly seek a hole or brush pile in which to conceal herself, but with foes on the ground she would depend upon her powerful legs to swiftly and erratically carry her out of danger and would only take to deep cover if there was the possibility of the enemy running her down. There was rarely that possibility.

Her one great failing, however, was an inability, if conditions were right for him, to detect a foe who might be lying in wait for her. If somehow he spotted her coming and crouched noiselessly, even though not well hidden, and the wind was in his favor — that is, blowing from the cottontail toward him — she might hop to within a few feet of him before sensing the danger and then it might be altogether too late. It was into just such a dire predicament that she was unknowingly moving now.

A small wiry dog, a brown and black mongrel with a predominant strain of fox terrier in him, had been trotting down the macadam road when ahead of him only a few dozen yards a gopher scurried across, a small flowing shadow in the early dusk, and in an instant he was in hot pursuit.

But the gopher — a thirteen-lined ground squirrel or spermophile — had not been quite as careless as at first it seemed. The little rodent had detected the dog at the same time the dog had spotted it, and now it put on a rather remarkable burst of speed, its short legs becoming blurred as they carried it swiftly into the short cover along the road just a scant dozen yards from where the nest containing the four infant rabbits lay concealed.

Despite its surprising speed, the gopher scrambled into its burrow only a few feet in front of the dog, disappearing into the small opening as if by magic. The frustrated dog shoved his nose into the hole and the hot scent of the little rodent filled his nostrils. As if he had suddenly gone mad, the dog began to dig with wild frenzy and for the first few minutes made such progress that it seemed he would surely unearth the small gopher very quickly. By the end of five or six minutes all but the hind legs of the terrier had disappeared into the excavation he was making, but the burst of energy had taken its toll and now he was growing weary and having to pause longer and more often to rest.

At last he conceded defeat and wearily plopped down upon the mound of cool fresh earth he had piled up, the dirt in his mouth and on his lips turning to mud as heavy perspiration dripped from the lolling tongue. For a long time he lay there resting as the dusk deepened and was just on the verge of continuing his aimless wandering down the road when the female rabbit hove into view.

Having satisfied herself that no enemy was moving nearby, the rabbit had now come along purposefully in a straight line to her nest from her final place of concealment. Her ears detected no sound from the dog and the wind was wrong for her to catch his scent. And concentrating now on the location of the nest just a little distance in front of her, she failed to observe the slight movement made by the terrier as he stopped panting, lowered his head and hugged the earth upon which he lay.

Straightaway she approached her nest and stopped only inches from it for one final inspection of the surrounding area. Her nose twitched vigorously and her ears turned slightly this way and that while her eyes scanned the sky and road, field and distant trees.

For a brief moment her gaze touched the shadowy form of the dog, but because he crouched perfectly still, she ignored him. Actually, most of her attention was centered above her, for in the open like this the greatest danger lay in attack from the sky rather than from the low grasses which afforded little camouflage to an enemy. Both hawks and owls hunted actively at this time of day.

At length, satisfied that danger was not present, the cottontail put her nose close to the ground and nuzzled aside a little mat of interwoven grasses and fur which covered the rectangular depression containing her four fawns — three females and a male. The depression had been dug by her a full week before her young were born and as soon as it had been made large enough to suit her — about five inches deep, seven inches long and five inches wide — she had cleaned the dirt from between the toes of her front feet and then lined the whole excavation with a layer of fresh grasses and green leaves.

And since this was her shedding season and much of her fur was already loose, she had plucked quantities of soft hair from her breast and stomach and added it to the nest as an inner lining atop the mattress of grasses. The result was an incredibly soft and comfortable little bed which she hid skillfully with the covering mat. An enemy not knowing its precise location would have had great difficulty locating it.

Eleven days ago she had given birth to her four offspring in the early dawn light only a foot from the nest. She had licked them clean of their mucous coating and given them their first meal of nutritious milk before one by one picking them up in her mouth as a mother cat carries her kittens and tucking them gently into the nest. There they had stayed until now, mostly sleeping and growing, actively excited only when she returned to feed them.

Twice in the past two days she had allowed them to leave the nest for a little interval in the darkness and they had chased one another and tumbled all over her gleefully. She had encouraged their nibbling of the tender sprouts growing nearby, but so far they had not shown any great interest in eating vegetation. Their mother's milk was far more convenient and tasty. But the outings had been brief ones and she had shown decided nervousness during these times.

Now, with the movement of the matting atop them, the young ones became animated. As always, after all day without food, they were eager for this first feeding of the evening. Their eyes had been open for four days now and tiny muted squeals of anticipation came from the fawns as she lowered herself over the depression so that they could reach her nipples and drink deeply of the rich warm milk she provided them — milk produced within her from the succulent grasses and plants she ate almost constantly, such as the slim and tender wheat sprout she had devoured only a short while ago.

These faint squeakings from the baby rabbits reached the ears of the terrier and he trembled with excitement. Unable to contain himself any longer, he abruptly leaped to his feet and dashed at the doe, but his reception was scarcely what he might have expected. She leaped to her feet at his approach, but instead of running from him as every other rabbit had ever done, she startled him by charging directly at him.

She swerved sharply as she reached him, narrowly missing being caught in the savage jaws that snapped at her. As she passed him she slammed both her hind feet into his face with a vicious kick. One foot caught the side of the dog's snout and did little damage other than to sting and anger him, but the other hit his left eye a fearful blow and the small claws on her foot laid open his eyelid in a painful gash and came uncomfortably close to blinding that eye.

So totally unexpected was the assault of this rodent, which everything in his instinct and past experience told him should flee rather than attack, that the black and brown dog was momentarily thrown off stride and bowled over. Before he had completely recovered his balance, the female cottontail was back again, rushing at him, nipping and kicking, and dodging fantastically to stay out of reach of the great teeth striving to close over her.

A year and a half ago this same female rabbit had been surprised at her last nest of that season by another dog — a gangly, rather awkward setter less than a year old who was considerably more curious than hungry — and using these same tactics she had successfully driven him off and later that night had carried her babies to a new place of concealment.

But the terrier blood was strong in this present hungry attacker and he had no intention of being bested by a rabbit, although for the first few minutes it appeared altogether likely that he would be. Kick after kick struck him, and some hurt enough to make him yelp sharply. Once the long incisors of the rabbit fastened on his lip and pierced it through, but he shook his head and tossed her spinning high into the air. She was somewhat stunned when she struck the ground and after that there was no doubt, if ever there had been, what the result of this battle must be.

Though her courage did not falter, her strength and dodging ability did, and with one heavy crunching bite across her shoulders and nape as she drove to the attack again, the dog crushed her bones and she died, with a final spasmodic kick.

The terrier retained his hold on the rabbit and shook her furiously a number of times and her head and legs flopped about loosely, as though she were no more than a piece of rag in his mouth. But after a little while he dropped her and shook himself as if he had been in water and then turned his attention to the nest.

With the memory of the preceding hunt for the gopher still relatively fresh in his mind, it was understandable that he did not stick his nose into the little nest but instead immediately began digging at it. And since it was so shallow, almost at once his ripping claws had pulled the young ones out, along with the nesting materials, dirt and debris, and flung everything through his hind legs into the deeper grass behind him.

At once realizing that he had unearthed them, the terrier spun around. One of the females, who was apparently injured by his claws, was crawling feebly nearby and he pounced on her and ended her brief career with a quick bite which severed her spine. Another was just scrambling into the heavier grass to hide herself when he nabbed her and the scene was repeated.

He then snuffled about in the grass seeking more and in a moment startled the third little female into a desperate run to escape, but he caught her handily and now only the male fawn remained alive of this rabbit family.

That final little member had been tossed nearly a dozen feet from the nest by the dog's furious digging and in landing one of his oversized hind feet had bent beneath him and though the leg had not broken, it was injured and he could not put his weight upon it very well. Nevertheless, he managed to squirm under a thick tussock of grass and there he crouched, his eyes bugged with fear and his little body frozen into immobility.

The terrier quickly lost interest in searching further and returned to his victims. He ate all three of the young females he had killed, holding their bodies on the ground with his front feet and tearing them apart with his teeth and swallowing them in thick chunks. His appetite was largely appeased by the time he turned to the dead mother and though he worried her still form considerably and ripped her carcass open, he ate little of her.

Satisfied at last, both with the hunt and with the meal, he picked his way back to the road and trotted nonchalantly off into the darkness.

VIII

THE TWELFTH DAY
OF MAY

F OR several hours the baby rabbit remained concealed in the tussock while the throbbing pain
in his hind foot gradually eased. The fear that had
so filled him also abated, and by shortly after midnight the hunger in him had become so great that he
limped out of concealment and instinctively headed
back to the nest site.

Though during the past few days he and his
sisters had tentatively nibbled at those sprouts near
the mouth of their nest, it was upon his mother's milk
that he still depended most strongly and which he
craved so much now. But the flow was permanently
halted.

He found her remains and, not comprehending the
torn limpness of her, he nuzzled up against her and

eagerly sought out a nipple. But though he found one, it was no longer firm and warm and filled with rich fluid as it had always been before. The flesh was cold and loose, and, though he tugged at it desperately, the milk failed to flow.

It was the movement he made, tugging at her, that caught the attention of the great horned owl flying silently thirty feet high over the fields. It wheeled sharply in midstroke and arrowed in to the attack. But it was still a dozen or more feet away when the little male rabbit sensed its approach and dived into the cover of deeper grasses. Instead of a living animal, the talons of the owl sunk into the lifeless form of the female, but this made little difference to the big bird of prey.

For fully three minutes it clutched the dead rabbit firmly, its stance a sort of crouch with wings still half spread, but then it relaxed and hopped onto the ground. Even though the cottontail's body had stiffened to some degree in death, the biting and shaking it had undergone from the dog had broken so many of her bones that the carcass was still limp enough for the owl to manage quite easily.

With some maneuvering, the large bird of prey took the rabbit's head in its mouth and began a series of gulping movements. At each such spasm a little more of the big female rabbit disappeared. After five minutes or so only the hind feet still protruded from the bird's mouth and then, after a final convulsive gulp, even they were gone.

The owl continued to sit on the ground here for half an hour, slowly turning its head or now and then preening itself. But at last it thrust itself upwards and the strong wings, laboring a bit more than when it landed here, bore it off in the darkness toward the trees rimming Oak Lake.

Only twenty feet away the little male rabbit crouched, shivering almost uncontrollably with fear and the hunger even more rampant within him. But as the minutes ticked into hours, the fear ebbed and the hunger dominated and at length he moved out of his hiding place in search of food. Within a short while he found a small patch of sweet clover and nibbled a new sprout, found it satisfying, and very quickly ate a dozen or more of the youngest and tenderest three-lobed leaves. A little farther along he encountered a growth of plantain and he tasted it, found it even more to his liking than the clover and devoured all but the oldest and toughest leaves of the weed. Despite his enforced weaning, it seemed he would survive.

But in nature, survival belongs to those wild creatures who possess a quickness of mind and body, and even they are often very hard pressed to exist: there is little toleration of carelessness, weakness or help-lessness in any form.

The little rabbit suffered all three.

Because of inexperience he would almost certainly become careless; because of the early weaning he was too weak; and because his principal method of de-fense — swift and erratic flight — was not only not yet well developed but was further hampered by the injury to his hind leg, he was virtually helpless.

Had the tragic incidents of this night occurred even as short a span of time as four or five nights later, he just might have been able to survive. But from the moment of his mother's death, his own likelihood of survival had become practically non-existent.

It was only a matter of time.

Through the remainder of the night he moved along aimlessly, occasionally stopping to dine on a succulent shoot of one kind or another. By dawn he had traveled to within several hundred yards of the big barn. Instinctively he had followed rabbit paths, stopping often to listen and sniff the air and now, tired from his night's wanderings, he hopped a foot or two from such a path and found in the short

pasture grass a section of discarded drainage tile —
a red clay pipe about three feet long with a diameter
of six inches which would give him plenty of room
inside to turn around.

It seemed an ideal place to hide for the day and,
except for one major flaw, it was. The single bad
thing about it was that the back end of the pipe was
blocked, clogged with mud that had dried and been
baked by the sun until it assumed a bricklike hardness.

The little rabbit sniffed the opening carefully,
detected no other scent than that of meadow mice,
and so unhesitantly moved into the pipe, turned
around and settled down facing the opening from
about a foot inside. If danger threatened he could
streak out of the opening and there was every reason
to believe he was perfectly safe.

So he might have been except for the big female
bull snake which thrust her way through the grasses
less than an hour later. She was an unusually large
snake, thicker than a man's wrist and fully eight feet
long. Her scales were large and thick, each with a
ridge or keel running down its center. The general
color of the serpent was a dull yellowish-tan, but all
down the length of her back and both sides were
indistinct rectangular blotches of darker brown. The

snout was rather sharply tapered and the long black
tongue, deeply forked on the end, flicked out and in
with an intermittent cadence.

The snake had been following the scent of the little
rabbit for more than a quarter-hour, having first
encountered the fresh, characteristic spoor along the
tiny path. The incredible sensitivity of her tongue as
it slid out of her mouth a considerable distance and
waved momentarily before being withdrawn had pre-
vented her becoming confused where mazes of inter-
secting paths had joined, and she had continued
unerringly on the correct trail.

In a manner of speaking, the snake's tongue had
"sipped" the air and detected minute chemical particles of scent the rabbit had left hanging in the air
or clinging to the grasses as it passed here. These
microscopic particles, picked up by the reptile's
tongue, were pulled back into the mouth and trans-
ported to a sensor called the Jacobson's organ for
analysis. Not quite an organ of smell and not quite
one of taste, the Jacobson's organ was something in
between, a superb combination of the two. In an instant upon finding the trail, the snake had accurately
determined the spoor to be that of a young rabbit
which had passed here not long ago. Had the scent
been that of an adult rabbit, she might have gone on

without following, but this was no experienced adult and so she had turned in the proper direction and begun to trail.

As she stopped about six feet away from the tile and sampled the air yet again, the spoor was so strong that the reptile not only knew the little rabbit was in the tile but, to within a fraction of an inch, just how far inside the tile he was crouched.

Her head lifted off the ground and for several minutes she swayed slightly and waved her tongue out for long periods at a time. Satisfied that the rabbit was thus far unaware of her presence, the snake lowered her head and slid silently forward, closing the gap. She kept herself out of visual range from the interior of the pipe until only inches away and then, with a swift coiling motion, abruptly blocked the exit and thrust her head deeply inside, jaws widely agape.

The little rabbit had no chance whatever. Not until that last quick movement when the snake blocked the opening did he comprehend the danger. Automatically he scrambled backwards to the farthest recess of the tile and then realized his serious error when he found he could go no farther. He pressed tightly against the caked mud at the rear.

Inexorably, almost casually, the snake's head fol-

lowed him. It poised for an instant to aim, and then
she drove her gaping jaws at the little rodent. The
rabbit virtually ran along the side of the pipe in his
frantic effort to get past that deadly head, but the
snake caught him across the hips and withdrew into
the open with him even more swiftly than the rabbit
could have.

The rabbit now squealed in mortal terror, a piti-
able wavering scream that carried far in the morning
stillness. He had time for that one squeal only, for
the instant they were in the open a series of heavy
reptilian coils wound around him in terrible compression while the jaws maintained their tight hold
on his body. The eyes of the little rabbit bulged and
his mouth opened and closed, but no further sound
came from him.

The constriction of the snake's coils was not meant
to crush the bones of the rabbit, but it was enough to
quickly and effectively suffocate him by preventing
inflation of the lungs. Death came very quickly.

Within a minute after the baby rabbit's struggles
had ceased, the big snake uncoiled and, without taking a fresh hold with her mouth, rapidly swallowed
the rabbit whole. It was an easy matter for her
because of the rodent's small size. More than once

she had swallowed large adult rabbits as well as full-grown rats which were far larger than the little cottontail that had just met his untimely end.

*   *   *

Immediately after swallowing the rabbit, the bull snake slithered into protective grass cover and moved along slowly until she lay outstretched beside a long piece of planking mostly hidden by grasses overgrowing it. For about half an hour she lay here quietly, seemingly lulled by the muted humming buzz of various insects being awakened by the first warm rays of the sun.

The swelling of her body several inches behind her head, which indicated the position of the swallowed rabbit, gradually moved farther back along her body, and by the time it had reached the midsection could only be detected with close examination. The only other movement she made during this time was an occasional flickering of her tongue as it tested the air.

At length her body rippled with a little spasm which began near her head and continued down the length of her body until it reached her vent area, about thirty inches from the tip of her tail. Her body in this area raised off the ground in a small humping movement and a compact cylinder of feces was ejected — not the remains of the newly swallowed rabbit, but the residue of a meal of three rats which she had caught some five hours before in a large woodpile beside the barn.

With the defecation function performed, she once again moved on her way, propelling herself along smoothly and with seemingly little effort. She held her head a half-inch or so off the ground, and it moved straight forward rather than swaying from side to side. Half a dozen inches behind her head began a series of curving movements which grew into wavelike convolutions down her body all the way to her tail. The wide flat row of parallel scales which lined her entire belly length expanded and spread apart as they moved forward with the curve of the body, always instinctively reaching out for some tiny projection — a pebble or twig or lump in the ground — against which to brace and contract and thus push her muscular body forward. So silently and smoothly executed was the process that it seemed she was swimming gracefully across the surface of the ground rather than crawling.

The bull snake is one of North America's four largest snakes, and although already over eight feet in length and easily one of the largest snakes in this whole geographical area of Oak Lake, she was not yet as long as she would eventually become if she survived. She was nine years old and, with luck, might live two or three times longer than that. And having reached her present size, there were very few natural enemies now against whom she might have to fight for her life.

One of the hazards she had overcome was being caught and devoured by the king snake, which would unhesitatingly attack and devour any other snake, venomous or not, up to a third its own length. But since the largest king snakes in this region just barely reached five feet in length, such danger had disappeared for her.

The same held true with most of the birds of prey native to the area. The various hawks that would have welcomed the opportunity to catch her when she was smaller — the red-tailed, red-shouldered, broad-winged and rough-legged hawks — would not attempt attack now when she might easily turn the tables on them and make them prey rather than predator. And even the rare bald eagle seen in these parts would tend to seek prey less dangerous to itself. Among the predatory birds, in fact, only the great horned owl still presented a menace of some degree; but as long as the rodents of fields and woods remained plentiful, the owl would be satisfied with them and not take any chances with the eight feet of tightly constricting coils possessed by this bull snake.

The only real dangers she faced now were dogs and humans and for these she was always on the alert, depending on both her eyesight and highly sensitive tongue to avoid contact with them at all times. And, especially during this past week, she had been placing even greater reliance upon her tongue and less on her vision. Where normally her tongue would flick out to catch scent and taste molecules still hanging in the air perhaps once every twenty or thirty seconds, now this sensitive organ was almost constantly testing the air.

The reason for this shift in defenses was apparent as she moved along steadily now. Over her eye, with its normally brownish-orange iris and large black pupil, had formed an opaque milky coating which, except for distinguishing between night and day and detecting the largest and bulkiest of objects, left her virtually blind. Yet, she showed no concern over it. This had happened at intervals many times over the years and would undoubtedly happen many more times in the future. It was merely the final change in her appearance before she shed her old skin for a new one.

And truly she needed the change. In numerous places on her body the old skin was nicked and looked ragged and her coloration was nowhere near as bright as it should have been. There was a peculiar loose dryness about it, too, which was foreign to her, for usually her skin clung tightly to her and was sleek and smooth and very clean, as if it were made of a plastic material — never slimy and becoming wet only when she entered water or passed through the dew-drenched grasses.

She moved purposefully now, heading back toward the barnyard and the pile of wood where she had caught the rats last night. Although she kept to cover as much as possible and crawled along the cattle yard fence rather than crossing the open barnyard, she ran into trouble immediately.

The same boy who had driven the tractor out the farm lane to get the flatbed wagon six days ago was just finishing his morning chores when he spied the big snake coming along the fence row. He had seen and caught many snakes in the past, but never before had he seen one here that was quite as large as this one.

Immediately he snatched up a pitchfork leaning against the fence and ran toward the reptile. He was still a dozen feet away from her when she detected him approaching, veered away from the fence row and slid out into the open barnyard, putting on a surprising burst of speed to get away.

She wasn't fast enough, though.

The boy pursued her, his long strides eating up the gap between them, and quickly he overtook her. He held the pitchfork raised in both hands as if it were a spear he was ready to thrust.

Realizing that she could not outdistance this pursuer, the bull snake stopped and coiled herself in a twinkling and raised her head a foot above the ground. Her tongue tested the air constantly and the heat sensors in it told her exactly where the boy was, though she couldn't see him well.

Probably no snake in the country has a hiss as loud or as demoralizing as the bull snake, and she made the sound now. It was a piercing, decidedly frightening noise, and as she made it she vibrated the tip of her tail rapidly against the ground, causing a muted drumming sound.

The boy jolted to a stop, suddenly extremely wary and more than just a little afraid. He had heard a few snakes hiss before, but never with such furious intensity. And the vibration of the tail against the ground perplexed and worried him. Could this be a rattlesnake that had somehow lost its rattles? He took a step closer for a better look and the snake suddenly struck out at him, missing him by more than a foot but greatly disconcerting him.

"Paw!" he shouted. "*Paw!*"

The farmer, a rawboned, rangy individual, rushed out of the barn at once, badly alarmed at the fright evident in his son's voice. But when he saw the cause he slowed and approached the boy more normally, the lines of concern leaving his face and being replaced by a broad smile which caused crow's-feet wrinkles to deepen at the outer corners of his eyes.

"Scared you, did he?" he said, dipping his head at the snake.

The boy nodded and tightened his grip on the handle of the pitchfork. "I'll kill him," he said, raising the implement to strike.

"You'll *not* kill him," his father said quickly, taking the fork from him. "Not while I'm here and not any other time, either."

"But why not, Paw?" the boy protested. "He's dangerous to have around. Maybe he's poisonous. Look at him! He tried to get me."

"Only because you scared him, boy. Any animal will try to bite you if he's in jeopardy. You ought to know that by now. And this isn't a dangerous snake at all. The other way around, in fact. Be hard to find any wild critter more welcome around here than one of these."

"Welcome?" The youth was incredulous.

The farmer nodded and walked slowly around the snake at a distance of about ten feet. He nodded again and repeated himself. "Welcome and valuable. You remember how your Uncle Harry had all that rat and gopher trouble on his farm near Des Moines?" He paused and reflected and then shook his head. "No, maybe you don't. You were just a little shaver then. Anyway, Harry's place was overrun with rats. They were into everything, especially the feed bins. And his pastures were alive with gophers. Holes and piles of dirt all over. He tried traps and poisons, guns, cats and everything else and couldn't get rid of 'em.

"Then," he continued, "some feller from the State Agriculture Department talked him into getting a couple pairs of bull snakes and turning 'em loose on the place. Much," he added, chuckling, "to your Aunt Molly's horror. Anyway, he turned one pair loose in the barn and the other pair out in the field where the gophers were thickest. I don't think Molly left the house for a month after that." He laughed again.

The boy was listening, wide-eyed, and after a pause to light his pipe, his father continued.

"Harry paid thirty dollars a pair for those snakes and Molly was fit to be tied about it. She thought it was the biggest waste of money she'd ever heard of, but I'll tell you something, son — and your Uncle Harry'll back me up on it, too — it was the best investment he ever made. In two years time, those snakes had just about wiped out both rats and gophers alike. He's still got a few, maybe, but nothing like before. And all because of some snakes like this one. Bull snakes, they are. Best critter a farmer can have around his place."

"But won't they bite you?" the boy asked.

"Oh, I 'spect they would if you tried to grab 'em," the farmer said, "but leave 'em alone and they won't bother you a bit. We're mightly lucky to have this one around and I hope there's some others around, too. I'd raise Ned with anyone I caught molesting 'em. Some folks do, you know, just because hating snakes is the thing to do. These bull snakes are too valuable for that kind of carrying on."

He squatted on his heels to get a better look at the bull snake, which was now quietly coiled, her head still slightly raised. Only the unusually rapid flicking of the tongue betrayed her lingering nervousness.

"You know," the man said, straightening, "I've seen a few rats around the place lately and I was getting worried about 'em, but if these fellers are moving in, they'll wipe 'em out fast. You'll see. He's really a big one, eh?"

"Sure is," the boy said, his voice cracking a little. "He kinda scared me. How come we haven't seen one around here before?"

"Oh, I've seen 'em — some smaller ones, anyway — out in the fields every once in a while. Mostly, though, they're holed up in the daytime and do their hunting at night or early in the morning. See that little swelling?" He pointed at the snake. "About midway along that outer coil? That's probably a rat he caught not long ago. And look at his eyes. See how milky? That means he's about ready to shed his skin. Wouldn't surprise me if you found it somewhere around here in a day or so. Well," he sniffed the air, "your mother's got the bacon on and I'm hungry. Let's go eat."

They walked away together toward the big farmhouse, the boy rather reluctantly and glancing back often. They had not gone fifty feet before the bull snake was in motion again, moving swiftly toward the big woodpile. She disappeared beneath it before the pair had entered the house.

Deep in the dim recesses below the pile she found a suitable hollow where some rats had piled up a quantity of dead grasses, bits of rag and other soft materials for nest-building and here she pulled herself into a loose coil and rested. She slept, and though her eyes were lidless and incapable of closing, her bodily processes slowed and even the nervous flicking of her tongue ceased.

And as she slept, the last of the little rabbit was digested within her.

I X

THE THIRTEENTH DAY OF MAY

For many hours the huge female bull snake slept deeply under the woodpile, and it was not until just after midnight that a desultory flicking of her tongue recommenced. At once her Jacobson's organ detected something that caused her relaxed muscles to stiffen and her head to poise alertly. The tempo of her tongue-flicking quickened and very quietly she drew her head back slightly, bunching the neck muscles preparatory to striking.

A faint sound came then, a light momentary patter accompanied by a slight brushing noise of fur rubbing against the tunnel walls. Dark as it was in here, eyes would have been basically useless in making out the large rat, even when it appeared suddenly at a narrow entrance to this larger hollow. Certainly the rat did not see the snake, but the snake's heat-sensitive tongue detected the rodent instantly, and as fast as thought, before the rat could catch the vague scent of the reptile, her head shot forward and her mouth closed over the animal's shoulders.

The rat squealed in abject panic and tried desperately to bite its attacker, but it had little chance. Almost as quickly as her head had gone forward to strike, the bull snake withdrew it, pulling the rat into the roomier quarters occupied by her body and at the same time throwing her thick sinuous coils forward. In an instant three or four loops had been wrapped around the rat, pinning it so tightly and effectively that its jaws could not open and the only appendage it could still move was its heavy hairless tail, which whipped about in a frenzy.

Now the bull snake exerted pressure and her incredibly strong constrictor muscles tightened unbearably over the rat, while her jaws retained their initial hold. The air was squeezed out of the rodent's lungs and the pressure kept those organs deflated. In less than a minute the big rat relaxed in unconsciousness, and a few moments later it was dead of suffocation.

The bull snake maintained her coil pressure for another two minutes and then relaxed her hold. This rat was considerably larger than the baby rabbit she had eaten this morning and therefore would prove a trifle more difficult to swallow. The problem was only a minor one at most.

She moved her jaws about until she had the animal's head suitably aligned in her mouth; and then occurred an amazing thing. Abruptly her lower jaw spread apart in front, the jawbone disconnecting at its leading edge and the elastic skin of her chin stretched taut until the row of back-angled teeth, which before had followed the unbroken arc of her lower jawline, now straightened and became two almost parallel lines of teeth. At the same time her quadrate bone — a complex hinged affair connecting her lower jaw to the skull at the back of her head — performed its double-jointed function. Normally bent in the center like the folded span of a large crane-scoop of a tractor, it now straightened, allowing the back of the jaw to drop almost as far from the skull as the front. The mouth of the snake had thereby become four or five times larger than normal.

As the sharp, recurved teeth held the rat firmly in place, she began ingesting it through the means of a curious series of movements. First one side and then the other of her mobile lower jaw moved forward and actually seemed to walk her mouth right around the animal. She wasted little time in the process and within minutes the large rodent had passed smoothly into her throat, leaving only the long naked tail limply hanging out. Then this disappeared even more swiftly as a series of convulsive gulpings and muscle ripplings thrust the prey far down the length of her body and into her stomach. Her mouth resumed its normal shape and she was immediately ready for another.

But now, instead of lying in wait, she actively took up the hunt. Moving smoothly and with only occasional pauses through the maze of corridors formed under the piled wood, her tongue continuing its constant sensing, she was very soon rewarded in her search. Ahead of her not more than a dozen feet was more prey; not just a single rat this time, but one adult and a half-dozen young ones. The young were not yet weaned, but they were already fully furred and quite large. All of them were still unaware of her approach and she remained motionless for a little while, as if planning her proposed assault on this assemblage — for this time she would not be attacking an individual animal, but rather seven at once and she meant to make the most of it.

At last she started forward again, very slowly. So silent was her movement that not even the sharp ears of the wary female rat guarding her family ahead caught any sound of the snake's coming. When the reptile's head had reached a point no more than a foot away from the nest and she had accurately pinpointed the exact location of the adult female as she lay nursing her six young, she stopped her forward movement but continued to let her body move up behind her and compress tightly for the forthcoming onslaught.

With dazzling speed then she shot forward, unerringly closing her powerful jaws over the female's back. The adult rat's squeals were echoed by the thinner, terrified cries of the young ones and there was a flurry of activity as they attempted to scatter in the darkness.

So quickly that she had not time to react in defense of herself or her family, the huge female rat was tied with heavy coils. The offspring, each of them about a quarter the size of their mother, had little room to negotiate during the initial frenzied activity. Two, in fact, merely crouched against the chamber wall, petrified with fear. Within seconds the bull snake had thrown loops about four of the young and was already constricting. One of the pair still loose escaped in a frantically screeching scramble down the entrance passageway, but the other ran into a cul-de-sac and huddled there whimpering piteously only a foot from the snake.

The bull snake paid no attention to it for the moment, concentrating on holding the four already in her coils while at the same time exerting the greatest pressure on the female clenched in her jaws and also enshrouded by coilings.

The larger rat struggled fiercely and at one point nearly succeeded in tearing herself out of the bull snake's mouth. But gradually her struggles weakened and then abruptly she went limp. For two or three minutes longer the bull snake maintained her unrelenting pressure of constriction and then she dropped the adult rat and, as if she had been waiting for this moment, her head darted into the blind passage and those savage jaws snatched up the fifth offspring. The tremendous pressure on the other four young did not relax during any of this activity.

At length, hardly more than five minutes after the initial attack, she began to feed. The young one that had been trapped in the closed passage and was last to be caught was the first to be swallowed. Its mother was next and, though it took the snake a certain amount of maneuvering to get her jaws positioned correctly around the larger animal, at last the right hold was achieved and her mouth began that awe-inspiring march around her prey. All this while the four young in the coils had been held tightly, and all of them were long since dead of suffocation. Now she released her hold on them and in rapid order swallowed them in turn.

She lay quietly again, peacefully digesting these seven rats she had swallowed since awakening — including the other adult captured a short while before. And though several times in the hours that followed she detected other rats moving cautiously in corridors nearby, she did not move except to be on the alert.

Her digestion of the rodents was relatively swift, and by noon the swellings of her body indicating her prey had shrunk through deterioration and compression until they were scarcely noticeable. It was then that she began a rather peculiar movement, pressing her nose to a piece of wood and rubbing it back and forth methodically. Before long the skin at the front of both upper and lower lips had loosened and curled away from the new underskin. The continued movement pushed it farther back until, with some maneuvering, she had freed her entire head of the old skin and it ringed her neck as if it were a frilled collar. Even the milky cover that had been over her eyes had gone with it.

She began crawling again, inspecting several passageways until she found a very narrow one that suited her, and here again she stopped to rub. Almost at once the loose skin snagged on one side of the passageway, and she moved forward slowly. Miraculously, as if she were peeling off a long rubber glove encasing her body, she slid out of the old skin. She went around several corners in the passageway and at each turn the old skin snagged anew and held and she continued to leave it behind.

The shed skin was quite elastic and stretched considerably and so it took a full ten feet of crawling before it had been pulled entirely free of her and lay strung along behind her, inside out but in one piece. Shedding the old skin seemed, as always, to sharply stimulate her, to fill her with a sort of exhilaration and now she quickened her pace and slid through the extensive woodpile passageways with amazing speed and agility and with little concern for the slithering noise she made.

In rapid succession she caught two more rats, both of them small and obviously only lately weaned. She killed and swallowed them without difficulty and continued her wandering. And finally, just as the sun was touching the horizon on the reed-choked bay of

Oak Lake's west shore, she came again into the open air.

If the boy who had seen her yesterday morning could have seen her again now, he would undoubtedly have been certain that this was an entirely different snake, so greatly had she changed in coloration. The general background color of her body was no longer a drab tan but instead a brilliant ivory-yellow hue, and the blotches and spots on her back and sides were clear and bright, a deep cinnamon shading into black, while her entire underside from chin to tail was a crisp fresh yellow.

But it was her head that had changed most. Her eye was now a striking brown with a definite orange cast to it, quick and flashing and highly sensitive to her surroundings. Invisible before because of the dry old skin, there was now a dark brown diagonal band extending from her eye on each side to the angle of the jaw and a parallel yellow band immediately above that. This gave her an appearance that was at one and the same time more rakish and more awesomely fierce. Finally, she seemed somehow even larger than she was before.

She moved steadily away from the woodpile and barn, heading directly for the large open meadow bordering the lane. Only once did she change direc-

tion slightly, to investigate a small cattle shelter.
The construction was little more than a four-posted
platform covered with a tin roof. This roof was
peaked and had, directly under it, a floored storage
area where there was room for perhaps a dozen or
more bales of hay. There was still plenty of room
beneath this for eight or ten or more cows to gather
and be sheltered from sun or rain.

The four corner posts were made of rough cedar
with the bark still attached where it hadn't been
rubbed away by back-scratching cows and, with de-
ceptive ease, she scaled one of them. By the time her
head eased up onto the hay platform, her tail was
still only a foot or so from the ground. She drew
herself up quickly and nosed her way through the
bales stacked here.

And at once she detected prey.

Following the lead of her tongue, she thrust her
head between two bales and startled a pigeon sitting
on its nest. With a startled cry and clatter of wings,
the bird shot away and only by the very slimmest of
margins eluded the strike of the bull snake. She left
behind, however, two nestlings. They were quite small
and, in fact, only now beginning to get their pin-
feathers. They would grow no larger.

The bull snake ate them in turn, alive, wasting no

effort in constriction or in turning them around in order to swallow them headfirst. The swellings they made on her body scarcely showed. She inspected this loft area a little further and then, satisfied that there was no other prey immediately available, although she detected the spoor of several mice, she spiraled her way headfirst down another of the posts and continued her passage through the meadow in the gathering darkness.

Twice as she moved along she entered gopher holes but neither time did she capture prey, although in both cases the gopher scent was so strong that it was obvious the animal had scurried out a back entrance and escaped upon hearing her approach.

It was as she neared the third hole that she abruptly stopped and raised her head high, her forked black tongue carefully testing the air. As she did so there was a movement at the mouth of the burrow and another bull snake began slowly emerging. It was a male, smaller than she by more than a foot, but a peculiarly aggressive animal.

There was no doubt that he had detected her at practically the same time and he approached her very smoothly, raising his head similarly as he neared her. When they were three feet apart he stopped and, facing each other, they held their upright poses for such a long time that they might have been frozen there. Only the tongues of both continued to taste and test the air.

Many long minutes passed in this extended mutual inspection and then the very tip of the male's tail vibrated excitedly against the ground. Three times in succession he lowered his head until his chin touched the earth and then raised himself again until his eyes were on a level with hers, nearly two feet high. Still, except for the waving of her tongue, she did not move.

The fourth time he lowered his head he did not raise it again but instead he moved forward slowly, slid gently along until he was two-thirds down her length and then deliberately crawled over her until he was entirely on the other side. When she failed to respond to this maneuver, he crawled under her once and then over her twice again in the same manner. On the last pass he loosely looped his body across hers in a series of waves and raised his head until they were neck to neck and head to head, looking in the same direction.

In this pose, with their heads still held quite high, both of them commenced crawling forward very slowly. As they moved he swung his head around behind her and then brought it forward again until

the side of his head was against the other side of her head and their necks were crossed. After a moment, during which he appeared to grow even more excited and his tail-drumming started again as they were crawling, he unwound from around her neck and then rewound in the other direction to repeat the odd process.

At last the large female began to show signs of sharing the excitement of the encounter. She raised herself higher and higher, her nose pointed to the sky, and he followed her lead until they projected upwards a full three feet high. Their muscles strained to force themselves even higher and the male, because of his shorter length, began to have a most difficult time. Increasingly he depended upon her for support, clinging to her front quarter tightly and leaning his weight against her. Still she raised herself higher, and at a height of almost four feet it became too much. She swayed, caught herself, swayed again and then tumbled back to the ground with him, in a jumbled mass of coilings. Three, four, five times his body swiftly coiled about hers and held tightly as she squirmed and writhed in an apparent effort to dislodge him.

After several moments the rough-and-tumble action subsided and they lay still together, resting. But a few minutes later they once again began lifting their heads, noses straight up toward the stars. Repeatedly they swayed and this time, although their necks were interlocked, their heads moved apart and both of them simultaneously moved their heads in a small circular motion within a diameter of about three inches. The strain of the maneuver became too much, and once again they tumbled over each other in a squirming mass.

This time when the frenetic activity abated, they lay nearly side by side except for the rear quarter of the male, which now nudged and pushed urgently at the female. She responded by raising that portion of her body slightly off the ground, and at once the male threw a coil under this loop and encircled her.

As if predestined — which, in a way, it was — their vents met and copulation commenced. Although she squirmed and twisted a little, it was the male who was mostly active now, looping and unlooping around her, pressing tightly against her or pulling apart. For more than half an hour this mating act persisted, and only gradually the tempo slowed. At last they lay still, their vents still joined, and for another quarter hour more they seemed almost asleep except for the desultory flicking of their tongues.

When they disconnected, the male resumed his

intertwining about her neck, but this time she paid no attention to him. She began moving off, slowly at first but then with increased speed, angling toward the farm lane where the grass grew thicker and deeper. He followed at once, but in a short while she was moving so swiftly that it was all he could do to keep pace a dozen feet or so behind her.

In the deeper grass she wove about with intricate and confusing movement patterns. He followed her persistently, no longer able to see her in the darkness, but his tongue working frantically to unwind the progressively puzzling maze of her passage. Twice she slipped abruptly into a dense tussock of grass and coiled there, and twice she moved out swiftly when it became evident that he would discover her. She then employed another tactic to shake off the tenacious suitor; she moved off in one direction just as rapidly as she could travel and gradually outdistanced him until she was thirty or forty yards in the lead.

Where a small erosion ravine intersected and a drainage tile went under the lane, she slithered down into the shallow water and followed it through the tile, then kept to the water for another twenty yards beyond the lane on the other side. Here she moved out of the water quickly, and ten feet away from it coiled into tight seclusion well hidden in dense cover.

The male did not appear again, having given up the pursuit upon emerging from the tile.

Fertilized now, the female would, in seventy or eighty days, lay up to two dozen eggs and perhaps even as many as thirty. They would be white with leathery, pliable shells, tightly adhering to one another and somewhat larger than hen's eggs. She would find a suitable place to lay them — probably in the warm decomposition of a rotting log — and stay with them, or at least in the near vicinity, for several days to make certain they were not disturbed. Then she would leave. About eight weeks later, incubated by the warmth of the sun and the decomposing wood and soil, they would hatch and from each would emerge a bull snake baby with a length of sixteen inches but almost exactly like her in every other respect. They would begin their own hunting immediately upon hatching.

But now, fatigued from her strenuous exertions with the male snake, she rested here a long while and continued digesting the two pigeon nestlings she had devoured earlier. It was hard for her to remain still for long, however, and within two hours she was on the move and hunting again.

She returned to the lane and moved along it smoothly, her tongue flicking rapidly and with sureness. Suddenly she veered to leave the lane, following a faint spoor to a hole not much larger than her own diameter. Without even a pause she entered it and followed its course as it angled downward for four feet and then leveled off. En route along this main passageway she encountered other tunnels leading off to small round rooms but she ignored them, knowing they were empty and continuing to follow the trail her tongue picked up.

She moved so swiftly through the passage that she was in the gopher's living quarters before the animal assessed the danger. She snatched it in her mouth headfirst and, since the narrow tunnel permitted no room for constriction, simply held on until the animal's struggles weakened. Even while it was still moving slightly, she swallowed it.

Next she turned her attention to the nest and methodically devoured in turn the eleven young which, at twenty days of age, were still ten days away from having their eyes open and were therefore helpless to escape her. Now they would never see daylight.

She emerged from the rear exit of the burrow, about twenty feet from the entrance, and continued her quest. By the time she reached the point where the farm lane emptied out onto the macadam highway, she had entered five more burrows and managed to catch and eat one more adult gopher and fifteen more young, all of them smaller than the first litter and from two different nests.

The night air had cooled considerably and now that it was almost midnight there was a noticeable difference in temperature between the air and the pavement. Throughout the sunny day the dark macadam had soaked up the solar heat and it still retained a good bit of it. The warmth felt pleasant on the distended belly of the snake and she stretched out to her full length upon it, parallel to and only a few inches from the edge of the pavement.

She lay there resting for a long while. Once an auto came whizzing past in the lane where she lay, but she was close enough to the edge of the road that it passed her with a safe margin and apparently the driver hadn't even seen her, for there was no slackening of speed.

Such wasn't the case when the second car came by. This one was in the other lane, coming from the direction in which the first car disappeared and moving considerably faster. But since it was on the other side, there was little likelihood that it would prove a threat.

The car swept past with a roar but almost instantly the brake lights flashed into life and the auto swayed precariously as it screeched to a stop. There came a fierce clashing of gears as the driver shifted into reverse and then the vehicle swayed violently again as it rolled backwards at considerably more than a sane speed. In a moment it had backed up beyond the bull snake and the reptile was now bathed in the harsh brightness of the headlights.

"Ha!" a man's voice shouted triumphantly from the open window. "I *thought* it was a snake. By gosh, honey, look at the size of that devil!"

"Ooh," cried a woman, her voice edged with fear and disgust, "kill it, Don."

"Well, you didn't think I was just gonna *look* at it, did you?" he replied sarcastically. "Sure I'll kill it. That'll be the third one this year. But the biggest one by far!"

He backed a little farther away and lined up his wheels so they'd be sure to strike the serpent. The bull snake, in the meanwhile, was becoming a little nervous, mostly because of the bright lights. Her tongue flickered out and in rapidly and her body began drawing together, preparatory to moving onto the shoulder and off into the darkness.

"He'll get away, Don," the woman shrieked. "Hurry up!"

There was another clash of gears and the car leaped forward. Both the front and rear wheels on the left side of the auto thumped over the snake and at once the vehicle stopped and backed up again, missing the snake on this move but lighting up the scene.

The bull snake was writhing in agony, her back broken in three places. She coiled and uncoiled, bunched into a tangle and straightened out, only to writhe pitifully again. For the second time the car jumped forward and the thumping of its wheels was repeated as it mashed her anew.

When the car backed up this time its lights showed a grisly scene. The snake was still writhing, though not as vigorously as before, mainly because her back had been broken in two more places and her stomach ripped open, its contents and her entrails crushed into the pavement.

A door of the car opened and the man got out and inspected the helpless reptile from a short distance away. He grinned widely and waved a hand victoriously at his female companion, who had no intention of leaving the safety of the car.

"We really clobbered him that time, Marie," the man said.

A spastic movement of the snake raised the head a little and the woman gasped. "Don, for heaven's sake be careful," she called in alarm. "He's lifting his head. He's still alive. He'll get you!"

"Wanta bet? You watch. I'll show you how I fix them so they never bite nobody again, you just watch."

He moved to the rear of the snake and tentatively reached out with the toe of his shoe and tapped the snake's tail. It didn't respond to the touch, nor did the head, which was continuing a pathetic rising and lowering as she attempted to make her crushed body respond.

Snatching the tail, the man lashed the snake over his head and slammed her full length into the pavement. There was a slight degree of muscular contraction in the reptile immediately following the hard smack of the impact, but that was all. Her head continued to move weakly on her broken neck. Determinedly the man grasped the tail again and this time, grunting heavily, snapped the snake as if she were a bullwhip. Three times more he did this without pausing, and when he threw the reptile down again her head had been snapped off her neck and her body lay still.

The man stood there for a little while, grinning broadly into the headlights and slapping his hands together triumphantly. Then he got back into his car, put it into gear and rolled forward over the bull snake's carcass a final time. He did not stop and the red eyes of his taillights gradually disappeared up the road.

The man was extremely proud of himself and the woman openly marveled at his bravery.

X

THE FOURTEENTH DAY OF MAY

S EVEN more automobiles rolled over the torn remains of the bull snake during the rest of the
night. Though one of them slowed momentarily, none
stopped. And in the first light of the morning, while
the remains were still recognizable as those of a large
snake, even someone familiar with the various species
would have been hard put to identify it with assurance. Except, of course, for its size.

The ants had come to the carcass first, during the
night. One had meandered past it accidentally and,
after some preliminary investigation and tasting,
had hurried off with his antennae waving wildly.
Within an hour there had formed a steady stream of
similar ants going to and coming from the remains.
Many of the insects had been smashed as cars con-

tinued to strike the remains, but this meant little to the survivors, who were intent upon their feeding and on the business of carrying bits of the meat and viscera away.

A number of moths had come, too, attracted by the sweetish smell of the mingled blood and body juices, and they flitted about the crushed mass, occasionally alighting and briefly feeding. Carrion beetles came also, a little later, equally attracted by the smell, and they hid under and fed on larger pieces of the body and laboriously pushed and pulled chunks larger than their own bodies off the road for burial, on which to feed later at their leisure.

With the daylight came bluebottle flies, a host of them, buzzing about noisily and much more interested in the partially digested contents of the reptile's stomach and the bloodier portion of the entrails than in the firm white flesh.

And then came a band of crows to the scene. A flight of seven of them, moving out on their first flight of the morning, homed in on the remains after sighting them from a considerable height. They squabbled among themselves as they picked and tore at the carcass, swallowing quite large pieces. A car that came by scattered them, but as soon as it had passed they came back and continued feeding.

One of these crows, a handsome, glossy black female, was chased by two of her companions a short distance when she flew off with a two-foot section of mangled skin, meat and bone. She dodged erratically to elude them and, since the pair were not really enthusiastic about the chase, they did not follow her far, deciding instead to return to the highway where it would be easier to obtain their own spoils.

The female continued to fly back in the direction whence she had come with the little band. This was toward a large woods south of Oak Lake and a bit more than half a mile distant from here. She zigzagged expertly through a screen of interlocking branches until she reached the medium-sized oak in which her nest was positioned. It was a clumsily built affair of loosely intertwined twigs in a sturdy crotch some fifty feet above the ground.

The five fledgling crows in the nest first heard and then saw her coming and instantly flailed their wings and cried out noisily in anticipation. These cries increased in both vigor and excitement as they spied what she carried in her beak, and the woodlot rang with the clamor they made. And as she landed on the thick branch a foot or so from the nest, a frantic scrambling broke out among the youngsters to get to the side of the nest closest to her.

Although they were fairly well feathered, they had not yet tried their wings and would not for at least six or seven days to come. But now, as the mother bird hopped toward them with the remnant of snake dangling from her strong black beak, they became so enthusiastic that the bird closest to her was forced onto the very edge of the nest, teetered there a moment with his tiny wings flailing ineffectively and then was sent spinning into space when accidentally butted by one of his sisters.

The little crow fluttered wildly, hit a branch a few feet below and clung for an instant with one foot and his chin while the stubby wings beat all the harder to regain balance. But the effort was too much and he fell again, badly off balance now, struck another branch quite hard with his left wing and cartwheeled all the rest of the way to the ground, where he hit with a bone-jarring thump. It was immediately apparent that he had injured himself. Though he regained his feet, his left wing hung all askew and his cries of hunger and eagerness had been supplanted by cries of pain and fear and bewilderment.

The mother crow dropped the snake remains into the nest among the four squabbling fledglings, who were not in the least disturbed about the disappearance of their brother. Then she skimmed quickly down to the ground and hopped to one side of her little injured one. She touched him with her beak, first on the neck and then on the broken wing joint, which made him flinch and cry more sharply in pain. Confused and concerned, the adult bird merely stood there and looked at her young one.

A short while later her mate appeared, also carrying a morsel of food which he thrust at one of the fledglings in the nest. When it was snatched away, he too fluttered to the ground and inspected his injured offspring.

The two adults walked around the baby bird gravely, soft cries of distress swelling in their throats. The injured bird was crouching pathetically now, and though he whimpered and moved his head to watch them as they circled him, he made no further attempt to move his body.

The fledglings still in the nest above continued their noisy din over the carrion for some time, but at last they quieted as the final torn bits of meat were swallowed. All this while the two adults had studied the situation here on the ground with mounting concern, occasionally resuming the intermittent marching around their injured offspring, occasionally touching or nudging him with their beaks, occasionally putting their own heads close together, as if in consultation. If anything, the young one became even less responsive.

After some time the male bird leaped up and flapped his way above the trees and then sailed off to the east. A few minutes later the female did the same, except that she angled northwestward toward the Oak Lake marsh. The little fledgling crow continued to sit where he was; hunched, frightened, and pained.

At intervals during the day the parent birds returned, never together but always with some morsel of food for the fledglings. Mostly they flew directly to the nest to feed the young still there, but three times the female and two times the male alighted on the ground beside the injured bird to feed him a cricket or morsel of bread, a piece of carrion or whatever else it may have found. But apparently the injured wing was not the only trouble with the baby bird, for though he did finally accept and eat one cricket late in the day, he ate nothing else and merely hunched in a sick and morose posture.

As evening came on, the male bird disappeared and the female returned to her nest a final time. She perched there nervously for several minutes and then dropped to the injured little bird, but he kept his eyes closed and remained wholly unresponsive. In a little while the mother bird shook herself, touched him gently with her beak as if in encouragement and returned to the nest to settle atop the young birds there for the night.

It was scarcely more than an hour after dark when the little crow on the ground awoke cold and hungry, with continuing pain, and he began to cry out pitifully. It was a soft, hurt-filled, whimpering sort of cry which carried far, and though the mother bird up above heard it, she did not leave the nest.

But several hundred yards away deeper in the woods another bird heard it and he did leave the perch he occupied. Scarcely a whisper of sound heralded his flight as he swooped easily through the dark woods like a great deep shadow. He darted through a tangled maze of outstretched branches without touching one of them and when he had reached a point he determined was close to where the plaintive sounds had originated, he landed lightly and just as silently on a low branch of a red oak. At this station he was no more than twenty feet away from the injured crow and only fifteen feet above the ground.

The little bird had lapsed into silence again — had, in fact, fallen asleep — and with neither movement from the fledgling nor the pain-laden voice to direct him, the huge great horned owl was unable to accurately pinpoint his prey. He sat very erect and utterly motionless, his great round eyes scanning the ground below, his ear tufts high and his muscles poised for instant flight. Not an inkling of noise betrayed his presence here and he was virtually invisible in the heavy darkness of the woods.

For fully twenty minutes he perched thus before his patience was abruptly rewarded. For the second time since nightfall the little crow awoke and made a faint peeping sound. Instantly the big owl's head swiveled toward the source and his keen eyes made out the little black shadow that was the bird. His wings unfurled slightly as he leaned forward but retained his perch. The injured fledgling murmured again, barely audibly, and like a shot the bird of prey leaped from the tree and sped directly to the spot.

High above, the mother crow heard the sharp cry of pain which was cut short in the middle and she knew full well what it meant. Parental love demanded that she fly down at once to her offspring's aid, but survival instinct overcame the impulse and, except to snuggle down a little more protectively over the fledglings in the nest, she did not move. While in daylight hours she would not hesitate to join a band of her fellows to harass this same owl, she knew that any detectable movement she made now could well be fatal for herself and her entire brood.

The great horned owl did not stay in the area very long. His powerful curved talons had sunk deeply into the little bird's body and there was only a brief moment of struggle before the small crow succumbed. A moment later the big bird of prey was airborne, rising smoothly above the trees and flying toward the northwest, his flight unhampered by the dead weight clutched in his feet.

He landed atop the broad flat stump of a tree someone had sawed down several years previously and at first he just sat there quietly, still clutching the crow. There were few enemies this large owl had to fear, but those few were enough and his vigilance never relaxed. The possibility was always there that when he landed, the spot he had chosen might be within range of the pounce of a great bobcat or the slashing attack of a dog or large feral house cat. From that time five years ago when he himself was a nestling, he had become ever more aware that relaxing one's guard was an invitation to disaster. His own existence, in large measure, depended upon other creatures relaxing their vigilance and falling prey to him.

But now, satisfied that no danger to himself was present here, he turned his attention to his latest prey. Releasing his foot grip on the little bird, he picked it up in his fierce curved beak by the head and held it just so for a moment. Then, with a smooth and decidedly well-practiced movement, he flipped his head back and gulped, half swallowing the fledgling in that single maneuver. His eyes partially closed from the expansion of his mouth to swallow the bird, he repeated the process and this time the fledgling disappeared altogether.

The owl hunched and swallowed a third time, blinked his great yellow eyes several times in succession, fluffed his feathers, preened his breast plumage with a series of rapid combing movements of his beak and then emitted a deep loud hooting which carried for well over a mile through the quiet night air.

A whole multitude of deer mice and meadow voles, flying squirrels and rabbits and other nocturnal creatures, on the move in the area nearby, froze instantly in alert, frightened positions, their ears ringing with the malevolent hooting of their dreaded foe. It would be a long time indeed before they moved again, and even a longer time before they ventured out into the open once more this night.

The owl, however, took to wing again immediately

after hooting and flew with strong measured wing-beats all the way across Oak Lake to the northeast bank before alighting in the skeleton of a long-dead elm tree.

For the first few seconds after landing he remained perfectly still on the chance that some sort of prey might be on the move below this tree, but when he detected no evidence of this, he fluffed his feathers and preened himself again briefly. Then he settled himself on the perch in a comfortable, somewhat slouched posture close to the trunk of the tree. Here he remained for several hours, seemingly asleep, but with his eyes and ears sharply attuned for further prey.

XI

THE FIFTEENTH
DAY OF MAY

THE great horned owl was an awesomely handsome bird and his fierce appearance caused him
to loom considerably larger than he actually was.
When his wings were outstretched they spanned a
full sixty inches, but when sitting he was just two
feet tall. With his stomach empty he weighed only
a fraction over four pounds, but it was rare indeed
that his stomach was empty for very long.

Right now, for example, in addition to the baby
crow he had swallowed an hour or so before midnight,
his stomach contained the remains of eleven mice, two
rats and a flying squirrel. That was only a start. It
was quite likely that before dawn arrived there were a
number of other inhabitants of this lakeside habitat

which would fall prey to his merciless sharp talons and strong, sharply curved beak.

He was a solitary individual, this owl, preferring to hunt and roost by himself except during the nesting season, which was now long past for his species. While all around him birds of every description were just now beginning to build their nests and lay eggs and most of the mammals had only a short time ago given birth to their offspring, his own mating had taken place months ago, in late January.

He and his mate, a strikingly beautiful bird larger even than himself, had then worked together to build their nest — a platterlike construction of strong twigs laced together in the crotch of a butternut tree just eighteen feet above the ground. There, at the close of the first week of a bitterly cold February, his mate had laid three large dull-white eggs and the two adult birds had taken turns incubating them. On three different occasions before the eggs hatched there had fallen heavy snows which had virtually cloaked the motionless bird in the nest. But they did not seem to mind this and when the snow buildup on head and shoulders became burdensome, they merely fluffed their feathers and shook it free.

All through the rest of the month the temperatures had been below normal, often dipping to sub-zero readings, but the warmth of the incubating birds kept the eggs safe. On the whole, except for making their hunting a little more difficult, the ill weather had little effect on the nesting of this pair of great horned owls.

On the face of things, it might appear that nature had played a strange trick on these huge birds of prey in causing their nesting to take place so early in the year, but there was good reason for it. After the eggs hatched, in late February, it was not very difficult for the parents to find sufficient food, mostly rodents, to sustain the nestlings. And when these nestlings became fledglings and had developed to the point where they could fly for themselves, when they could begin their own hunting and be abandoned by their parents, there was very little likelihood of their suffering from hunger despite their limited hunting ability, since by that time the woods and fields were alive with young rabbits and mice, baby woodchucks and rats and gophers, all of them greatly inexperienced themselves in avoiding danger. Had the fledglings been hatched later and not left their nest until early or middle May, the young mammals would have become more adept at looking out for themselves and food would have been harder to come by and survival for the immature owls considerably more difficult.

It was well over a month now since his three off-spring had sailed away to take up their own lives and his mate had flown off to the northeast to establish a semipermanent residence in a deep woods of her choice. There was little possibility that he would ever see any of them again, his mate included, but this concerned him not at all. Solitude was a way of life with him and, except for annual reproduction, he lived with but one purpose dominant in him — to satisfy a virtually insatiable appetite.

He considered this area fringing Oak Lake as his own private hunting grounds and would unhesitatingly attack any other owl — even other great horned owls — which might encroach on his territory. More than once screech owls, short-eared, long-eared and barn owls had fallen under his attack and been devoured by him.

This territory was one he knew extremely well and, while he did not make it a habit to perch or roost in any one place exclusively, there were a dozen or more particularly favored locations which he frequented, either while hunting or while sleeping. This very skeletal elm tree in which he now sat along Oak Lake's northeast shore was one of those perches he liked.

About an hour after midnight, when he was just

on the verge of flying off to hunt elsewhere, a movement on the shoreline beneath the tree caught his
attention and he cocked his head to watch intently.
There was little moon and the starlight was weak,
making the night particularly dark, but such was the
light-gathering power in the pupils of his huge eyes
that objects were as clear to him now as they might
have been to a human being on a heavily overcast
afternoon.

He had no difficulty in spotting the pair of young
muskrats playing carelessly in the shallow waters
beside a steep mud bluff some twelve feet high. They
chased one another in and out of the water, tumbled
over and over together and generally had a rollicking
good time. They were completely unaware of the owl
watching them patiently, waiting for the most ideal
moment to strike. He could easily get one of the
muskrats at any time, but he wanted them both, and
so he waited.

Time after time his muscles flexed preparatory to
flight as the young animals scampered dangerously
far from the water, then relaxed as they scampered
back. The pair grew increasingly lax in their watch-
fulness and soon were scrambling high atop the bluff
and, much as otters at play often do, sliding down
the steep bank to splash into the water, swim under

the surface to a lower bank some twenty feet away, and repeat the process. And each time they slid, the bank became slicker and the slide faster and more exhilarating.

At one point the pair left the water about the same time and tumbled about on shore until they had reached the top of the bank. One of them immediately plunged off and splashed noisily into the water below, but the other remained on top. It was at this instant that the great horned owl shot from his perch.

With no warning sound preceding him, he dived to the attack and plucked the small muskrat off its high bank before it even knew it was in danger, before it had any opportunity to voice an outcry. As if they were daggers, the talons dug through the soft flesh and found the heart and the little muskrat was dead before the owl had carried it a dozen yards.

The bird made a wide circular sweep and returned to the dead elm, alighting on its lowest remaining branch, holding the perch with one foot and bracing the body of the little muskrat against it with the other. He sat still and watched as the other muskrat again scrambled up the bank and stood erect at the top as he looked for his companion. In another moment he had slid back into the water to seek him there.

Bending over, the great horned owl took the head of his victim in his beak, threw his own head back and in four great gulps swallowed it. He blinked his eyes slowly as the meal settled and then silently leaped from the perch again.

The second little muskrat had once more emerged from the water and clambered up the bank, still searching about in a bewildered manner. This time it strayed twenty or thirty feet from the edge in the quest for the lost companion; it was a grave error.

He saw the owl only an instant before the bird struck, and he leaped frenziedly to one side. The jump was neither far enough nor fast enough. The talons of one foot raked its shoulder and back and then lodged in the hip, and there was a brief desperate struggle accompanied by an agonized screeching from the little rodent.

Flapping his large wings to maintain balance, the great horned owl grabbed with his other foot and the powerful leg muscles drove the curved claws deeply into the animal's body and its struggling ceased. Moments later the little muskrat was reunited with his lost companion for a final time.

For a considerable while the owl remained on the ground here, his eyes half closed while rapid digestion was taking place within his stomach. It was nearing dawn when again he took to wing and sailed smoothly across the eastern end of the lake to the southeast shore. Here, in a dense grove of cedars where he frequently roosted, he settled in one of the largest trees, close to the trunk and about a dozen feet above the ground.

He slept here throughout the day and when he awakened just before sunset he relieved himself of a great mass of feces. For some minutes after that he sat hunched in a peculiar manner until, with a strong bodily spasm, he regurgitated an oval pellet about the size of a large hen's egg. The process was repeated twice more and each time a pellet of comparable size was regurgitated and fell to the earth below.

It was a remarkable process, for each of these pellets contained fur, feathers, skulls and other bones of the creatures he had previously swallowed whole. Within his stomach these indigestible materials had been drawn together, rolled and compressed into tight pellets and finally regurgitated. And at once the owl was hungry again.

His hunting activity this evening centered in the low prairies and partially marshy meadow ground to the east of Oak Lake. This was the habitat of a great population of meadow mice, along with a scattering of deer mice. But despite their numbers here, they were not easy to catch because their tiny paths tunneled beneath the grasses and formed a complicated network of passages into which they could disappear in a wink. Nevertheless, by flying just inches above the grass and plunging the instant he saw one, he managed to catch eight mice in a couple of hours, though he missed many more than he caught.

This fatiguing form of hunting burned a great deal of energy and so, after a few more near misses, he sailed off toward a scattering of farms to the east. And at once he detected prey. Thirty yards or so from a farmhouse were a number of small pens, and a movement near them attracted him.

The animal was so large that at first he took it to be a huge cat or small dog, but as he settled to the screening atop one pen, he saw that it was a very large domestic rabbit that had somehow escaped its confinement. Within the pens there was a flurry of scuffling as the rabbits there took to cover in the warren boxes, but the big rabbit outside merely froze in place.

The owl hesitated. This rabbit was easily four or five times the size of the usual cottontail and surely it weighed twice as much as he, if not more. But though he had never tackled anything quite this large before, it took only a moment for him to decide to do so now.

He catapulted himself from the pen top and caught the big rabbit in the midst of its first bound as it tried to flee. One set of talons dug deeply into the animal's back and the other set caught the back of its head. The strength of the rabbit was considerable and there was a melee of flapping wings and kicking legs punctuated by a loud terrified squealing from the rabbit.

For some time the outcome of the conflict was in doubt, but then one of the owl's talons punctured the base of the skull where the spine attached and the rabbit stiffened and then went limp and it was all over.

Before the big bird even had time to contemplate how he would eat this great meal, there came a fierce yapping and a beagle hound bounded onto the scene. It ran into considerably more than it had anticipated. Reluctant to lose his hard-won prey, the owl held himself in readiness atop the rabbit, and when the charging dog was only a few feet away he flapped his wings to maintain balance and thrust his outstretched talons directly into the startled dog's face. One claw punctured the beagle's noise painfully and another on the same foot tore the upper lip. The opposite foot snatched the dog's muzzle and one of the talons missed an eye by only the very slightest of margins.

The bird held on tightly, beating his wings and slapping the dog's head and shoulders with them. Thoroughly startled and distinctly hurt, the beagle fell back and tried vainly to get its teeth on the bird. But with nose and lip being ripped, the wing-beats hitting him like hammer blows and the beak of the bird ripping through his ear with excruciating pain, the dog quickly lost his initial enthusiasm for the affray.

Throwing himself on his side, the beagle thrashed about wildly, kicking his feet at this terror and biting constantly but finding nothing but air between his teeth. A series of pained yelpings erupted from his throat, and with that a powerful yard light suddenly bathed the whole area in a bright glare and a door slammed.

Finding himself quickly getting into a position of vulnerability, the owl released his hold and sped off into the darkness, low to the ground. Behind him, growing fainter with distance, the yelps of the beagle continued. The dog would hereafter be a bit more reluctant to attack large birds.

The owl alighted in a hickory tree to rest and the

rapid beating of his heart quickly returned to normal. While he never deliberately sought out such encounters, this was the second time he had bested a dog much larger than himself but lost his prey in the process. His feathers were not badly ruffled, but he preened them carefully and remained quiet for a long while. His exertions had burned much energy and he would rest fully before continuing his hunt.

A few minutes later he was asleep.

XII

THE SIXTEENTH DAY OF MAY

T HE night was more than half over when the great
horned owl awakened, relieved himself and then
regurgitated a pellet containing the fur and bones
of the mice caught earlier in the evening. Those eight
mice hadn't done much to appease his great appetite
and so now, ravenously hungry, he flew to the south-
west, passing the edge of the lake and his cedar grove
without pause.

He flew for nearly two miles before coming to a
large sprawling farm in a state of considerable dis-
repair about three-fourths of a mile due south of the
lake. The unpainted barn was partially collapsed
and the roof of one shed was almost blown away.
Fences were broken and various pieces of farming
equipment littered the ground. The house needed

paint badly also; and there were two gaping holes in its front porch. Except for the neat little garden plot behind the back door and some dew-heavy clothing hanging limply on a much-knotted clothesline strung from house to tree, the farm might well have been abandoned.

There were rats here in great numbers, scores of them moving boldly in the open or in and out of the deeper shadows of the outbuildings. There was a cluster of perhaps eight or nine of them by the little hen coop and even more by the dilapidated corn crib. They seemed little concerned with the possible danger in so exposing themselves and, as if he had known it would be so, the owl swept onto the scene in a long glide which ended in the agonized squeal of a rat being punctured by the great talons.

As if by the wave of some magical wand, every rat vanished at the sound and the barnyard became devoid of life except for the owl. With accustomed ease he swallowed the dead rat headfirst and then flew to a perch atop the corn crib. Within ten minutes the most daring of the scattered rodents were reappearing. They emerged hesitantly at first from their hiding places, but quickly became bolder when they detected nothing to fear. After fifteen minutes more the owl swooped again and almost the identical tableau was reenacted.

Not until this peculiar cycle had been repeated five times at increasing intervals did the barnyard rats finally appear to comprehend the nature of the danger that awaited them and become more wary. It had grown light with the dawn now and their numbers had begun to thin anyway as many scuttled off to their hiding places for the day.

Daylight did not particularly inconvenience the great horned owl, even though other owl species were distinctly bothered by it. In fact, this big owl frequently hunted in the daytime, especially if the skies were heavily overcast.

At night the pupils of his eyes expanded until they were very nearly the diameter of a dime, with very little iris showing, but in daylight these same pupils contracted until they were little more than pinpoints of black in the center of large, brilliant yellow irises.

So now, though daylight had come and the sun was on the verge of appearing, he continued to hunt. Two more rats fell prey to him just as the edge of the sun appeared above the field to the east, and perhaps others would have, except that the last one squealed very loudly for a considerable time before dying and a tousled head appeared at one of the windows of the house.

A moment later the door was flung open and a barefoot man clad only in long underwear bottoms plunged outside with a shotgun clutched in his grip. The owl had perched again atop the corn crib and was just preparing to swallow the now dead rat, holding it in his beak by the scruff of the neck.

At the disruptive appearance of the man, the big bird launched himself into the air and flapped ponderously toward the lake, his flight considerably slowed and clumsied by the weight of seven rats in his stomach and one held in his mouth.

The blast of the shotgun shattered the early morning stillness and hot pellets of lead plucked at the big bird. A burst of feathers from him filled the air and he faltered in his flight, dropped the rat he was holding and then regained control and continued to fly northward with all the speed he could muster. Another shot followed the first, but this one was a clear miss and then he was out of range.

Pain was a living fire in him, emanating from various parts of his anatomy. Seven of the pellets had struck him: two of them had ripped out long furrows of feathers on his back and slid under the skin and lodged there; one had punctured his right

side quite deeply, tearing into vital organs; two had punctured the thick thigh muscle of his right leg and come to rest deep in the flesh; one had burned its way through the flesh and feathers of his right wing close to his body; and a final pellet had lodged painfully, but not dangerously, at the base of his neck.

He flew a half-mile before stopping briefly in a dense tamarack thicket where he regurgitated everything in his stomach, including a quantity of his own blood. His weight lightened by almost half through this measure, flight was easier but no less painful to him. He continued falteringly toward the most secluded spot he knew, the grove of cedars along the southeast shore of the lake where, the day before, he had perched.

With uncommon difficulty he landed in the same tree where he had roosted yesterday. He moved in awkward and painful sidesteps until he was close to the trunk of this tree and then he leaned against it with his right side, favoring that leg and supporting his weight with the uninjured left leg.

Each of the pellet injuries throbbed with its own individual pain, but the agony caused by the single pellet that had punctured his left side, tore through the stomach lining and lodged in his liver blotted out the minor fire of the others. A dark, viscous blood dribbled slowly from his side and his great yellow eyes closed with the pain of it.

Occasionally his beak opened and closed as a sharp spasm struck him, and a time or two he shivered uncontrollably for several minutes at a stretch, nearly losing his balance as a result. But at last a great drowsiness overtook him, numbing the pain, and he became still. He fell asleep and was still in this same comfortable slouch against the tree trunk when a boy stepped into the little clearing directly beneath him.

*   *   *

The boy had been in the woods since before dawn and he was well armed: not with gun and ammunition but with camera and film, with thick sketch pad and a pocketful of pencils. He walked slowly, frequently stopping and letting his eyes search the ground and trees and shrubbery ahead of him. Less than fifty feet from the tree where the wounded owl was perched he stopped and sat on the ground for ten or fifteen minutes while he made a series of quick sketches of a fern frond that was half unrolled.

When he began walking again, his eyes were on the ground searching for something else to sketch and he was soon directly beneath the big owl's perch without even suspecting the bird's existence. That is, until he saw the pellets.

At first he thought they were raccoon droppings and he knelt for a closer look. But when he identified them an instant later his heart leaped and at once he looked upward and saw the huge bird, still leaning against the trunk of the cedar with his eyes closed, only seven feet over his head.

A wild but controlled excitement blossomed in the boy and his fingers trembled badly as he readied his camera, fearing that any instant the big bird would fly off before the image of him was preserved on film. It was by far the closest he had ever come to a wild great horned owl and his cup of happiness was brimming at such good fortune.

The light was poor at best here in this copse, but there was enough for some reasonably good shots and he took them swiftly, inwardly fuming at the loud click each time the shutter snapped and expecting at any moment to see the bird open its eyes and take wing.

He snapped pictures from beneath and from all sides, and when his roll of film was used up he quietly laid his camera to one side and unlimbered his pencils and did a whole series of rapid sketches, marveling all the while in the immense good fortune that had befallen him, not only in coming upon such a bird but in having it sit still for him for such a length of time.

But when, after he had worked feverishly there for an hour and the bird had still neither moved nor opened its eyes, a perplexed frown furrowed his brow. He took a stance a dozen feet from the tree, pad braced well and pencil poised to catch that moment of awakening, the initial opening of the wings, the swiveling of the head, the opening of the great orb eyes. And then he called aloud:

"Hey!"

The bird did not move and, surprised, he called again, more loudly. "Hey, owl. Wake up! Move!"

There was no response, and for the first time the youth sensed something seriously wrong. He lay down his sketching equipment, walked to the cedar tree and slapped the trunk so hard that his fingers stung. Still there was no reaction from the owl.

The boy scanned the surrounding area quickly and his glance fell upon a long thin dead branch. He went to it quickly, picked it up and broke off the smaller twigs projecting from it until he had a slender pole ten feet in length in his hand.

Gently he raised it and touched the very tip of it to the bird's breast and, when this failed to rouse it, he tapped slightly harder. The bird moved then, but not voluntarily. It tipped backward slightly, balanced precariously for a moment and then tumbled to the ground.

The great horned owl was dead.

Mouth agape, the boy simply stared for a long while, not believing what his eyes were witnessing. And then a flood of questions filled his mind. Why? How? Did it die there? Did someone put it there? Was it poisoned? Was it somebody's elaborate idea of a way to trick him?

One of the owl's eyelids had been pulled open with the fall and already there was a distinct glaze over the iris and pupil. The boy tossed his stick aside and dropped to his knees beside the bird and carefully put his hands under it and picked it up. It was not as heavy as he had expected and he turned it over slowly, inspecting it.

The blood had only begun coagulating and it stained his hands. He sought its source and found it and then he found several of the other places where the pellets had entered and then all at once his own vision swam and tears coursed down his cheeks.

He put the bird on the ground and wiped his eyes with the back of his hand, suddenly ashamed of his tears and fearful that someone would see him and make fun of him. But a deep sadness welled within him, and his lower lip trembled again as he studied the carcass before him, so noble even in death. And along with the sadness came an anger at anyone who could so senselessly, so needlessly destroy such a magnificent wild creature. A bitterness he had seldom known created a bad taste in his mouth, and he momentarily lived a little fantasy in which he encountered the person who had done this and made him everlastingly sorry for the wretched deed.

He stayed in the cedar copse most of the morning, at first making a dozen good close-up sketches of the bird or parts of it. He sketched the head, the beak, individual feathers and toes. He studied the coloration carefully and made notes of the subtle changes of color where they occurred and finally, when he had done as much as he could in this respect, he opened his pocketknife and very carefully began to skin the bird.

Although he had never killed a bird and never intended to, he had at his home an impressive collection of study skins. Most of them were songbirds — wrens and robins, larks and thrashers, vireos and warblers — but there were a good many others among them; a few hawks and a screech owl, several species of woodpeckers, a shrike, a bobwhite quail, red-winged and rusty blackbirds and, of course, grackles and starlings and sparrows.

All of these were birds that he had found dead. The majority of these had been killed by autos; others he discovered beside the railroad tracks. Still others he had picked up, especially after severe spring or autumn storms, at the base of a thousand-foot-high television tower not very far from his home.

Each of these birds he had skinned with great care, always dusting the inner side of the skin with a combination of alum and arsenic powders to prevent insect damage, then padding the body cavity with cotton batting and placing a label on the foot which bore the date and place of discovery along with the common and Latin name of the species and the bird's sex.

These skins were an invaluable aid to him in his art, for only through minute study of them was he able to detect and emulate in his oil paintings and watercolors the subtle nuances of hue and shading in the plumage. And yet, even though he needed them badly, it never failed to distress him to skin out such a bird, and with unfaltering regularity the thought came to him while he was in the process of skinning one that he wished the bird could suddenly come to life, unharmed, and dart away from his hand to the freedom of the wilds to which it was hatched.

Because he worked with slow care it took him over two hours to complete the skinning of this great horned owl, but he had done an excellent job, especially in those areas where the skinning was made particularly difficult by the lead pellets having torn the flesh. When he was finished he tore three sheets of sketch paper from his pad and taped them together edge to edge with transparent tape from the roll he had long ago made it a habit to carry in his pocket for emergency repair of accidentally torn sketches. He now had a large cylinder of paper, and one end of this he sealed together with more tape. Careful not to disrupt the plumage, he then placed the owl head-first into the open end of the paper cylinder and sealed it behind the bird.

Satisfied that his newest specimen was now relatively safe from accidental damage, he turned his attention to the carcass. Once again he sketched, and this time it was the muscle structure of the bird that he drew, for this too would prove of value to him in properly shaping further great horned owls he might paint.

When he had finished with these he laid his equipment aside and used his pocketknife to dig a hole in the soft loam beneath the tree in which the bird had died. Into this he placed the carcass and covered it, tamping down the soil firmly so that it would be less likely to be unearthed by any scavengers. He then walked down to the lakeshore, thirty yards distant, rinsed his hands and knife and found a large round stone which he carried back and planted solidly atop the center of the little grave.

He felt better now that all this was over, and he began collecting his gear preparatory to leaving when a thought struck him and he set everything down again. Remembering what had first attracted his attention to the owl, he recovered the pellets and sat cross-legged on the ground as he dissected them.

They were firmly packed gray oblongs, easy to open. Fur and a few feathers were the binding materials holding them together in such compact bundles, and when he opened them he found a wide range of bones which he studied carefully. Here he identified the skull of a squirrel and another that was undoubtedly that of a baby crow. Two other skulls might have been squirrels or, for that matter, young woodchucks or muskrats. Two others were obviously those of rats and there were a number of mouse skulls, most of them with the lower jaw disengaged.

The multitude of bones — tiny femurs and ulnas and tibias, pelvises and vertebrae and ribs — were in such a hodgepodge tangle that they were valueless to him, but the skulls he found very interesting and he put some of them in his pocket for closer study later on. He only took two of the mouse skulls, those that were in the best condition, and he discarded one of the muskrat skulls and that of the fledgling crow, as both of them were heavily damaged.

When he left the cedar grove, there was little indication that he had ever been there at all: a small mound of freshly packed earth, a small boulder, a discarded stick . . .

. . . and a neat little pile of bones and fur and little black feathers.

*　　*　　*

During the afternoon and evening there were several visitors to the cedar grove, but only two of them — a bird and a mouse — paid much attention to the pile of dissected owl pellets.

First to come was a rangy, battle-scarred house cat, which padded into the little clearing with every indication of continuing on its way without pause. But then a vague scent touched its nostrils and it stopped, sniffed and accurately followed the scent trail to the tree. Here, on the surface of the ground beneath the limb upon which the owl had died, the cat found and smelled at length several coagulated drops of blood. It looked around slowly for their source but saw no creature. A little curious but not really particularly aroused, it circled the tree once, sniffed at the spot where the boy had skinned the great horned owl and again at the boulder beneath which the remains were buried, but then continued on its way.

Next to come was a dainty little pine warbler, a pert, sparrow-sized, olive-colored bird which flitted nervously among the upper boughs of the cedars before finally fluttering to earth beside the small heap of pellet debris.

She cocked her head first to one side and then to the other as her bright little brown eyes took in this scattering of fur and bones. She flicked her tail several times in excitement. Not more than thirty yards away, where a cluster of pines rimmed the cedar grove, she was building her nest and what she saw here suited her purposes ideally.

The nest, about twenty-five feet up in one of the pines, was a neat little structure of well-woven rootlets and leaf stems, stringlets of bark from wild grapevines and a lacing of tent-caterpillar webbing skillfully interwoven to the fibers to help withstand the buffeting of winds whining through the pine needles. It was a strong nest and was practically completed at this stage, needing only a few finishing touches. The fur from the pellets was precisely what she wanted to complete the job.

She hopped lightly into the midst of the pellet debris and her head bobbed up and down rapidly as she picked up and flicked away the tiny bones intermingled with the fur. She was particularly interested in the longer guard hairs which had once cloaked the little muskrats that the owl had eaten, and in a short while she had a large tuft of them clenched tightly in her sharply tapered, dark brown bill.

With a decidedly nervous style of flight she flitted away to her nest and worked rapidly there, stuffing the fur into various niches and gaps in the fiber construction. Seven times she returned to the pellets for more fur. When she was finished scarcely a hair remained among the scattering of little bones and her nest was now warmly lined with that fur — all over the inner bowl form and even covering the entire lip of the nest. The baby warblers that would hatch here would be as cozy as if they had been hatched in a fur-lined muff which, in effect, was exactly what the little nest had become.

For a long while after that the cedar copse was quiet. No other creatures came by until late in the afternoon when a mother skunk with five tiny offspring in single file behind her ambled past a dozen feet away from the owl tree but did not stop. A bluejay flying by overhead caught a glimpse of the stark whiteness of the little bones, wheeled sharply in midair, spiraled down, investigated, lost interest and just as quickly departed. As the sun was setting, a medium-sized toad hopped slowly but purposefully across the clearing and vanished toward the lake, only to be followed ten minutes later by a sinister-looking hog-nosed snake following doggedly on its trail.

Not until late dusk, however, did another visitor show interest in the remains of the pellets, but the interest this one showed was pronounced. She was a woodland deer mouse, a delicate, attractive little creature even though obviously heavy with young. She was seven inches long from the end of her nose to the tip of her tail, but practically half this length was the tail itself.

Streamlined, sleek and very dainty, she had short

fur which was a deep rich reddish-brown on back and sides, and her entire underside, from chin to end of tail, was an immaculate white. All four of her feet and her lower legs were white also, giving the illusion that she wore stockings, and a set of unusually long and sensitive whiskers sprouted from each side of her muzzle. Unlike the house mouse with its unattractive small beady eyes, this deer mouse had quite large and distinctly intelligent eyes and they, in harmony with the oversized ears which were lined with more of the white fur, gave her a curiously appealing expression.

She entered the small clearing from the west with her nose twitching rapidly and moved directly to the scattering of bones. Stopping first at the skull of the baby crow, she sniffed at it for some time and then nibbled at it experimentally. The skull was still fresh enough to be chewable and it was very rich in vital calcium, and since this was just what her body chemistry was demanding at the moment, she chewed away with vigor at the skull.

When she had finished eating a rather remarkable portion of the crow's cranium, she then engaged in carrying the other bones scattered about — except for the heavier skull bones — to a dead tree some forty feet away. Here she carefully deposited them deep in a natural crevice near its base. The job took over two hours to finish and she was exhausted when she was done. She remained at the tree where she had hidden the horde and squeezed into a little chamber behind some loose bark and made herself comfortable.

Almost instantly she fell into a deep slumber.

XIII

THE SEVENTEENTH
DAY OF MAY

Not until shortly after midnight did the woodland deer mouse awaken; immediately she scurried out of her hiding place and away, in a series of rapid jumps which carried her effortlessly into the surrounding darkness. She was an extremely nimble little creature and often leaped unexpectedly a surprising distance to one side or another, as if to throw off any would-be pursuer or foil the aim of an unseen plummeting owl.

Angling toward the shoreline of Oak Lake, she traveled steadily until reaching a dense clump of alder and willow scrub. Here she expertly scaled a slender sapling, which swayed a bit with her weight, and then she disappeared inside a ball of grasses as large as a man's fist about two feet above the ground.

Last year this had been the nest of a cardinal, but some weeks ago the deer mouse had moved in and remodeled it until it was no longer recognizable as a bird's nest. Using long dry grass stems she had cleverly roofed the abandoned nest over, lapping and relapping the dry blades until the ball shape was the final result. The only opening now was a tiny round door low on one side and this is where she entered.

Within the nest were five other deer mice. One of these was her mate and the other four were their offspring. The latter, even though nearly adult size, were still nursing. They greeted her with a chorus of thin, high-pitched squeaks which quickly degenerated into a somewhat shrill buzzing sound with a rather fetching musical quality to it.

She touched noses with the male and then, though the young ones were obviously intent on nursing from her, for the moment she refused herself to them, forcing them back from her with nose and front paws and chattering at them incessantly. Frustrated in their endeavors, which heretofore had always been highly successful, several of the young now began thumping the floor of the nest very rapidly with their front feet, causing a rapid drumming sound characteristic of the species when excited. Irritated by this display, she silenced them with several well-directed nips.

When at length the minor bedlam in the small nesting chamber had ceased and the young ones had reluctantly settled down, she began to cleanse them with her tongue and, after a moment, the male moved to help her. Most wild animals keep themselves clean, but few devote as much attention to maintaining personal cleanliness as the woodland deer mouse — an extremely fastidious creature which spends much of its active period each day cleansing itself or others.

But this cleansing the female mouse was engaged in now seemed vaguely different somehow from those given previously. There was an unusual urgency to it, and the reason soon became apparent. With the job completed, she touched noses with her mate a final time and disappeared out the doorway. She would not return to them or to this nest again.

Since their birth, thirty-five days ago, these young ones had been nursing. Had she chosen to, she could have weaned them fully a fortnight ago, but she had indulged them and they had continued to nurse from her, though with a marked decrease in fervor and need during the past ten days than previously.

She had given birth to the four of them alone in the bird's-nest house she had reconstructed, but a few days after the arrival of the young ones she had been joined by the male. Only two weeks after their birth, when their eyes were still closed and would not yet open for another four days, her mate had impregnated her again, and all during these last three weeks a new litter had been forming within her. Now it was time for their arrival and she would not tolerate the presence of others at such a moment. Perhaps her mate would find her again in a few days, perhaps not. It made little difference. If he did not show up, another male eventually would.

During her outings over these past few days, the female had been constructing a new nest, this one built beneath a large arched chunk of bark well hidden by undergrowth on the forest floor. But though the locale was entirely different, the nearly completed nest was similarly constructed — a ball of dry grasses and shredded vegetation, in the center of which was a hollow lined with plant down. And, as with the other nest, there was a small opening low to one side leading to that hollow.

She could, perhaps, have ousted her family and remained in the converted bird's nest, but in the process of raising that family the nest had become soiled and was distasteful to her, and she welcomed this change. It was not unusual for her species to change residence three or four times a year, and only very rarely were two litters ever dropped in the same nest.

She moved about with a display of efficiency in the new nest area now, collecting a bit of soft grass or plant fluff here and there and carrying it to the new home. Not until long after sunrise did she give the entranceway to this nest a final approving patting with her front paws and enter the cozy inner chamber to sleep.

Highly experienced as she seemed to be, it might have been thought that this female was a rather old mouse or at least one who was well into the adult span of her life. She was not. She herself had been born less than one hundred days ago not very far from here, one of a litter of six.

Unlike her own offspring, she had been weaned at sixteen days and was mature in twenty-eight. Fourteen days later she had mated and conceived, and on the sixty-third day of her life she had given birth to her first litter — the same litter which just last night she had abandoned for good.

She had finished construction of this fresh new nest beneath the chunk of bark none too soon. Her sleep was fitful and several times she whimpered faintly. The sun was at its zenith when the brief stabbing pains of labor began, and by the end of an hour she had six new babies, each greedily sucking the milk she provided.

They were not an especially attractive sextet. Their skins were entirely hairless and in color a bright pink, almost red. Bluish lids were tightly sealed over bulging eyes and their mouths were only barely large enough to encompass one of her tiny nipples. Each of the babies was only an inch and a half in length, including a tail much shorter than the body — a ratio which would soon change. By the time they were weaned, the tail of each would match the body length or even exceed it.

She washed the six tenderly with her tongue, frequently picking one or another of them up in her front paws to reach and clean underside areas. Barely audible pipings of sound came from them as they squirmed under her ministrations, and as soon as each was released he wriggled instinctively back to the warmth of her side.

Twice more during the afternoon she nursed and cleaned them, and it was growing dark again when she left the nest and scampered along a faint trail through the undergrowth. About twenty-five yards from her nest she came to a small hole in the ground, into which she disappeared without a pause. Ten inches below ground level the sloping tunnel branched off into two rooms, both of which were crammed with a variety of seeds. Most of these were weed seeds, but there were also a few oat and wheat grains and quite a large number of the tiny seeds of blackberries and the pits of small fruits — apricots, papaws and persimmons — and a large number of nuts, predominantly hickory nuts.

This was the abandoned store of some other mouse or chipmunk that had long since met its fate somewhere and upon which the deer mouse had accidentally stumbled in her explorations. To these stores she occasionally added her share. When she found an unexpected source of seeds or nuts she would immediately cram her cheek pouches so full that it looked as if she suffered from a severe case of mumps. Then she would carry her treasure to this storage depot. If something happened to her, then eventually another mouse or chipmunk would discover the horde, use it and add to it; and so the treasure was passed along often through many generations of small rodents.

When her outside activities were hampered through the need of caring for her young, as now, the female woodland deer mouse could come directly to this lode and eat her fill leisurely without having to burn up a great deal of energy in seeking new food.

This is what she did now, devouring quite a large

number of berry seeds first, followed by a dozen or
more apple pips which she expertly husked with her
sharp incisors. Satisfied for the moment, she left the
tunnel and returned through the heavy darkness to
the nest to feed her young again.

As soon as she touched the entryway the babies
inside began whimpering and she lost no time in
getting to them and settling down so they could feed.
When they had drunk their fill from her, during
which time she napped, she washed them in turn and
then, once again hungry herself, left the nest.

Almost at once upon emerging from beneath the
piece of bark she encountered a huge cricket, and the
chase was on. The insect bounded away in great
erratic leaps but she followed it with uncanny skill
until, twenty feet from where the chase originated,
she pounced upon it and slew it with one sharp bite.
She perched on her hind legs and sat very erect,
balancing herself with her tail. She held the cricket
between her front paws as if she were preparing to
eat an ear of corn. Abruptly she crammed the whole
insect into her mouth, chewed and swallowed vigorously until it was all gone.

In another moment she was on her way again. She
chased another cricket but lost it and minutes later
pounced upon a moth that had alighted near her food

cache. After eating it all except for the wings, she entered the chamber and ate some more seeds. Then she washed herself carefully and headed back to her new family again.

Twenty feet away from her nest she froze.

A large skunk was in the act of tearing up the nesting site. He ripped away the protective bark and snuffled about eagerly until discovering the ball of nesting materials. He shoved his nose deeply into it and then, suddenly very excited, tore it apart with his front claws and successively found the six new-born young where they had dropped. He devoured them as he found them, as if they were no more than beetle grubs.

Petrified, the mother mouse watched as the skunk continued to sniff about, looking for more. After several minutes of fruitless searching, the black and white mammal relieved itself on the spot where the nest had been and continued rather noisily on its way and was quickly gone in the darkness.

XIV

THE EIGHTEENTH
DAY OF MAY

THE female woodland deer mouse had remained where she was for quite a long while, and it was well after midnight when she stirred again. Her movements were hesitant and showed considerable trepidation. She hopped back and forth in the scattered ruins of her nest, and a faint querulous sound whispered from her throat as she sought any of her babies that the skunk might have missed, but there were none. She drummed her front feet on the ground in agitation and at least half a dozen times leaped high into the air for no apparent purpose.

When she had grown very weary from these exertions she finally calmed down and without further delay left the disrupted area, following a tiny trail which led toward the lake. Although she drank water only rarely, gathering most of her moisture from the seeds, berries and insects which made up her diet, now she was quite thirsty and so she went directly to the shoreline and drank deeply.

Here and there in the predawn darkness large bullfrogs were calling back and forth, and from not too far away the unmelodious croak of a great blue heron sounded. The sounds frightened her and sent her scurrying into a nearby patch of cover. Both bullfrogs and herons, she knew, would eat her if she blundered into their range. Safe in the cover, however, she crouched beside a large stone and rested for a while.

The past night had been an extremely busy one for her, and she was uncommonly tired. If the skunk had not torn up her nest and eaten her young, she would have been back there hours ago, probably sleeping soundly as her babies drank their fill from her. If she had another nest to go to now, she would have gone there at once, but she had none except that converted cardinal's nest which she had deserted earlier; once abandoned, a nest was never returned to.

But such speculations were out of her realm. She had no nest now and, until she constructed another, she would sleep wherever the need struck her, as at this place. Very likely she would begin construction of another nest immediately upon arousing from this sleep.

It was, however, a time of misfortune for this little mouse. Her sleep was as deep as it ever was under normal conditions and she did not catch the slight sound or movement that suddenly came about six feet away from her dozing form. A little mouselike creature superficially similar to herself but considerably smaller stood high on its hind legs and sniffed the air quietly.

A vague scent of the deer mouse touched the animal's nostrils and he stiffened; his tiny, sharply tapered snout twitched excitedly. He moved a little closer, stopped and sniffed again.

Now he had the location of the mouse pinpointed and he became extremely cautious, moving slowly and without the faintest hint of sound. He stopped often to listen and sniff the air, alert for even the slightest suspicious indication that his quarry was becoming alarmed.

This was a masked shrew, one of the most rapacious creatures in nature and, for its size, among the fiercest. Weighing less than one-fifth of an ounce, he was shorter than three inches in body length, generally a drab brownish-gray in color and having a yellow-brown tail only a bit over an inch long. His

head was greatly elongated and so distinctly tapered
that it appeared conical. His ears were very small,
almost hidden as they lay flat against his head, and
his eyes were so tiny that they were nearly invisible
without close scrutiny.

When he had advanced to a point no more than
eighteen inches from the deer mouse, his mouth
opened and closed several times, exposing a set of
vicious-looking front teeth. They were very sharply
hooked teeth, much longer than they were wide, and
each of them was bright red on the tip, as if permanently stained by blood.

At ten inches from the sleeping mouse he stopped
again and his muscles tightened. The tip of his short
tail trembled with excitement and, as if fearful that
the slumbering mouse would hear it, he abruptly
spurted forward, covering the remaining distance in
two bounds.

The deer mouse heard him coming on the first
jump and awoke with a start, but by then it was too
late. Before she had a chance to react, the shrew had
catapulted himself into her and the red-tipped teeth
had sunk deeply into the immaculate white throat.

A strangled, piercing squeal erupted from the
mouse and she tumbled over and over in a desperate
effort to dislodge her attacker, but the shrew clung

tenaciously. For nearly a minute the battle raged, but the hooked, forward-projecting teeth of the shrew had found the jugular vein and severed it, and in moments the woodland deer mouse was dead.

Breathing rapidly from his exertions, his heart hammering at the rate of over thirteen hundred beats per minute, the shrew released his hold and spent several minutes cleansing the fresh blood from his breast fur. This finished, he methodically ripped the mouse apart, devouring her brains and internal organs with phenomenal speed and then starting in on the meat.

Fur and bones he flipped aside as they got in his way, and in an amazingly little while the entire hind quarter of the mouse was gone. But now he was sated and moved a few inches away to once again wash his front paws and chest and snout. And then, without even another glance at the mouse remains, he scurried away just as the first glimmer of dawn began streaking the eastern sky.

*   *   *

No creature inhabiting the fringe of Oak Lake led a more frenetic existence than the masked shrew. He seemed to live in a state of constant overexcitement. His movements were always swift and very nervous and he seemed utterly incapable of remaining long in one spot.

Such a temperament was exhibited now by the shrew after leaving behind the remains of the deer mouse he had slain. Although he had eaten very nearly an amount equivalent to his own weight, his digestion was so swift and his need so great that before he had traveled more than a few hundred yards he was becoming very hungry again.

During this distance, mostly covered by short spurting runs punctuated by occasional erratic jumps for no apparent reason, he had stopped perhaps twenty times. At each stop he closed his eyes and was instantly asleep, a state in which he remained for anywhere from ten to ninety seconds. At each awakening he relieved himself of more waste materials and then moved on, and so it was little wonder that now, hardly an hour after eating the deer mouse, he was again actively hunting. The fact that it was now full daylight did not at all bother him. Night and day were alike to him and he was active around the clock. Only once or twice daily did he drop into a deep slumber which lasted for an hour or more, and from such slumbers he always awoke with a frightful gnawing hunger in his stomach and began the search for more food without delay.

Though his eyesight was poor, both his hearing and sense of smell were keen and these, along with actual touch, were the senses that most often dictated which way he should travel. Habitually he kept to the mouse trails, and so he did now, following them through deep grasses or undergrowth and often going underground in them. Every now and again he would pause and sniff very loudly, as if he were blowing something from his nostrils, and then he would utter a series of high-pitched squeaks, almost as if he were urging himself on to even greater effort.

Every once in a while he paused and cocked his head to listen for the faintest of scratching, audible only to his ears. When such a sound would be heard he would move about nervously, listening and sniffing until he had located the exact spot, and then abruptly he would dig with wild abandon until he had uncovered the worm or grub or subterranean insect that had caused the noise.

Occasionally when he came across seeds he ate them, and berries he would consume with gusto. And though he found none now, he would eat his fill from any carrion discovered. He was, in short, a walking appetite and, as such, was utterly relentless in tracking down a wide variety of living creatures ranging in size all the way up to a young rabbit or squirrel

— animals which were easily ten or more times his own size.

But the mainstay of his diet was mice and insects, and these, especially insects, he ate in enormous volume. If enough food was available he could eat up to several times his own weight daily, and if it was not available he could starve to death in as short a time as six hours.

Had he been capable of growing as large as a raccoon or cat he might well have become the fiercest and most dangerous animal on earth, but the fact of the matter was that his species was among the smallest of the mammals in the world and had a very short life expectancy.

At birth he had weighed so little that it would have taken more than two hundred individuals like himself to weigh a single ounce. He had been born along with four others just three months ago and already he was middle-aged. Life at such a high-strung pace as the shrews lived it did not invite longevity. At eight months he would be very old; and at a year, ancient. Only with extreme luck would he live to see two winters.

In the twelve weeks of life that he had already lived he had learned that food to his liking was most abundant close to the edge of Oak Lake, and therefore much of his wandering and hunting was done here. Beetles, flies, bees, mayflies, butterflies and a wide variety of other insects attracted to the water's edge fell prey to him constantly, and woe betide the frog or lizard, spider or small bird which failed to sense his approach and flee at once.

Three hours after eating his fill of the deer mouse — during which time he snacked on four beetle grubs, an earthworm, a large moth and a tiny spring peeper frog — he encountered a young meadow mouse and pursued it some thirty feet along grass-walled passages before it made the fatal mistake of plunging into a blind tunnel. There he cornered and killed it much in the same manner that he had slain the deer mouse.

This mouse was not much bigger than himself and when he finished feeding there remained of it only a messy little clutter of bone and bits of fur, along with the skull and one complete hind leg. And now, after cleaning himself thoroughly, he slept deeply. His breathing slowed from a normal eight hundred fifty breaths per minute to a mere five hundred and his heartbeat diminished to only ten pulses per second.

When he awoke, just over an hour later, it was as if he had never been asleep. Exhibiting the same nervous energy which characterized his every waking moment, he was asleep one instant and the next had leaped to his feet and raced out of the little tunnel as if pursued by a horde of devils.

A dozen or so feet from the little tunnel he had just vacated he plunged into a long hollow log just in time to avoid being snatched up by a plummeting sparrowhawk. The bird came to a jarring halt and stared with some bewilderment at the ground where the shrew had just been and where by rights its talons should have impaled him, but didn't. The colorful little bird of prey shook its head in agitation and leaped up and away with an angry shrieking. Not very often did it miss like this.

At the other end of the log the shrew peeped out tremulously, his nose twitching rapidly. He hesitated only a few seconds before spurting off into heavy cover and continuing his hunt. Already the bird was forgotten. His nervous dartings carried him back to the water's edge, and he ran along it swiftly. A leopard frog leaped out of his way with only a fraction of an inch to spare and plunged into water three feet from shore. Except for the briefest of pauses, the shrew paid little attention to it.

Ahead of him seven or eight feet there was a thick raft of lily pads which came within a foot or so of shore. On the closest of the pads a cluster of half a dozen yellow sulphur butterflies had alighted, attracted by a sweet sap oozing from a crack in the surface of the broad circular leaf. Between the glossy pads and shore the water was strangely muddied, and a lumpy rock projected a little way above the surface.

The shrew leaped to the rock and scurried over its ridges to the far side. From this vantage point it was still about six inches to the lily pad, and the little animal paused uncertainly. He could swim well enough but he preferred not getting wet. The choice was not his, however, as suddenly the rock moved beneath him and then submerged, leaving him afloat some eight or nine inches from shore.

He had made a fatal miscalculation, for the rock was not a rock at all but rather the rugged shell of a snapping turtle. He swam frantically for shore and safety, but at last this was a race he lost. With a lightning thrust of the head, the turtle snapped him up and knife-edged jaws almost cut him in two.

With the shrew's head and front quarter still projecting from her mouth, the turtle turned and swam out into the deeper waters of the channel. She settled in a small clearing on the bottom and remained motionless for several minutes, her eyes closed.

At length she gulped and swallowed, and with that the shrew was gone.

For some minutes more the turtle remained where she was, and then she turned and came back to shore and entered a tangled cluster of cattail reeds growing in a little covelike indentation where a tree had once been rooted but was now many years gone.

In the thickest portion of these cattails, where the water was only mere inches deep, she stopped. Dead reeds cloaked her rough back, which now projected from the water again, and she rested her chin on a submerged cluster so that her eyes and nostrils were out of the water also; and in that position she slept all day.

*　　*　　*

With the coming of darkness the large female snapping turtle became active again and moved back out into the channel to hunt. At once she detected the unmistakable scent of carrion, and inexorably she followed it up, moving southeast parallel to the shoreline. She traveled over two hundred yards before coming to the source of the water-borne aroma — a large carp lying dead in the shallows.

There was no indication of what had killed the fish, but with this the turtle was unconcerned, unlike the many reptiles which prefer to kill their own prey and rarely or never touch carrion. She pulled herself through the shallow water to the carcass, scattering the host of minnows and crayfish that had been feeding upon it, and herself began to eat of it.

She fed slowly, almost mechanically, her parrot-like jaws cutting out great wedges of the tainted flesh and swallowing them. Gradually the water here became very muddy as she braced her front feet against the carp to give herself leverage to rip away the meat.

By the time she had eaten her fill half the night was gone. Ponderously she crawled out into the deeper waters and began to walk slowly along the bottom, conspicuously careless of what other creature might see her.

XV

THE NINETEENTH
DAY OF MAY

T HE big snapping turtle had little concern about
the other inhabitants of Oak Lake. No creature
in these waters had fewer natural enemies or more
nasty temperament than she and the others like her.
She was twenty-three years old and quite large, well
over two feet long, and weighed in excess of forty
pounds. She was, additionally, a potential hazard
to every living creature in these waters.

Other than man himself, there was no creature
here who could harm her, and having safely reached
adult size, she would undoubtedly continue to prowl
these bottoms until she died of old age, perhaps at as
distant a time as a score of years from now. Provided,
that is, that she did not run afoul of her greatest
enemy — man.

She was by no means afraid of the human animal and, if it came to that, would attack him savagely. But she respected him and the danger he represented to her and therefore made it a point to scrupulously avoid contact with him at all times.

Twice over the years she had been caught on hook and line, but both times she had broken free and the hook still stuck in her jaw had eventually rusted away. Another time, without even realizing it, she had come within a hairsbreadth of falling into a barrel-type turtle trap in the sprawling marsh at the other end of the lake.

But beyond doubt her closest encounter with a human came about when she was thirteen years old. A boy of about ten had spied her back projecting from shallow water near the edge of the marsh and he had splashed in and dragged her ashore by her long tail. It might well have been the beginning of the end for her, but the boy became careless and held her too near his leg and suffered a badly torn calf muscle when her fierce jaws closed on him. He had screamed and dropped her and then yanked himself away, leaving a chunk of his flesh in her mouth and scarring his leg permanently. And as he had hobbled away crying and bleeding, she had turned, tanklike, and reentered the water.

She was by no means the largest snapping turtle in Oak Lake. At least a dozen others resided here who were as large or larger than she. One of these, in fact, was easily double her size. This was a tremendous, ugly old creature with heavy mosslike algae coating his upper shell, his weight certainly in the neighborhood of eighty pounds. But that old male spent virtually all of his time on the bottom of the lake, either moving about slowly in search of carrion or else very cleverly concealed and awaiting whatever hapless creature might come within range of his savage strike.

This female, on the other hand, spent a major portion of her time roaming the lake's shallows, where there was always an abundance of frogs, snakes, smaller fish and other life upon which to feed, such as the shrew she had captured yesterday. But though she preferred the shallow fringes of Oak Lake, only rarely did she ever leave the water entirely, for on shore she was clumsy and relatively slow and at such times decidedly vulnerable to her great human enemy.

She was by no stretch of the imagination an attractive creature. Some of the turtles living in this water, such as the terrapins and painted turtles, had pleasant characteristics — glossy shells that were very smooth, often with intricate whorled patterns on upper or lower shell or both, along with brilliant red or yellow stripes and blotches on head and neck and legs.

Not so the snapping turtle.

Her huge wicked-looking head and broad neck were much too bulky for complete retraction into the shell as with other turtle species. Her legs and tail, too, with great rolls of flesh around them where they joined the body, could only be drawn in slightly. Her lower shell, in truth, was not much of a shell at all but more just a shield which covered her vital organs and was nowhere near as large or protective as the upper covering. That upper shell was ridged and ugly, a nondescript gray in color and, toward the rear of it just above the tail, the edge was serrated in a series of points.

Her tail was long, gradually tapered, and along the top of it had grown a crest of upright enlarged scales somewhat like those an alligator has on its tail. Both her upper shell and the top of her tail had begun to accumulate a coating of the mosslike green algae which, if it didn't improve her appearance, certainly was extremely effective in providing camouflage for her.

And as if to add a final touch to her overall

unpleasant appearance, at least a dozen small black leeches had taken up their blood-sucking residence on the exposed flesh of her underside at the points where legs, tail and neck joined the body. Of these parasites she seemed wholly unaware.

Her eyes could only be described as awesome. There was no softness about them but rather a sort of constant cold calculation. They were small, with tiny black pupils and speckled black and gray-green irises — eyes that were set high and close to her nostrils so that if she desired she could stretch her long neck and raise only nose and eyes above the water surface. When she did this, as she often did, in the marsh areas where matted vegetation floated on the surface, she was so camouflaged as to be invisible.

Her whole shape and color, in truth, lent itself to being superbly camouflaged, and it was on this characteristic that she depended in large measure for capturing her prey. It had come as no surprise to her when the shrew had run onto her back, taking her upper shell to be a rock. A mouse or two had made that mistake previously, as had several frogs and marsh birds. In most cases they learned too late the error of their judgment.

As was her custom after catching prey or eating some manner of carrion such as the dead carp she had just eaten her fill of, the snapping turtle now wandered casually along the bottom. Several times if she had exerted herself she might have caught prey; once a large bullfrog with legs dangling in the water above her beside a raft of lily pads; again when a young muskrat swam right past her as she lay quietly on the bottom. But she was pleasantly full with the meat of the carp and paid little attention to these smaller creatures other than to note their presence.

She moved along very slowly for a long time, and when the water began to grow brighter with the growing daylight, she once again settled down to rest in a little pocket along the shoreline where the water was four feet deep. Every hour or so she rose to the surface for air, but then resumed her rest on the bottom and did not become active again until the middle of the afternoon.

She went to the surface for air here in this little pocket a final time and then resumed following the channel back along the lakeshore toward the marsh. She continued to move unhurriedly along the bottom, walking rather than swimming. Although she could swim well enough if the need arose, her weight was such that it caused her to burn a great deal of energy, and she was not inclined to so exert herself.

Most of her traveling by far was done along the bottom in this manner, and though it was not a rapid form of movement, nevertheless she could cover great distances doing it.

During her twenty-three years of life here in Oak Lake there were few areas of the bottom she had not walked across at one time or another — sometimes in water as deep as thirty or forty feet, often where the water was as shallow as only a few inches, but most frequently a short distance from shore in water ranging between four and twelve feet in depth.

Now, as always when she walked the bottom, a cluster of little fish paced her. They kept a quite safe margin between themselves and her head, keenly aware of and greatly respecting the speed and accuracy of her strike. Mostly these fish were bluegills or small bass, but occasionally larger fish of the same species, along with perch, carp and spotted gars, fell in with the procession and followed her. They knew that when she found prey, as eventually she would, particles of the creature she tore apart would drift away from her, and upon these they could feed.

After traveling over one hundred yards she stopped, well hidden, in a thick growth of water weeds beside a sandy clearing in five feet of water. During all this distance she had risen for air only once, though she had been submerged for over an hour. If necessary, she could remain below the surface for two hours or more without feeling any great discomfort and, if she were merely lying in wait instead of actively roaming the bottom, this submerged time could be very nearly doubled.

She remained in this spot for an hour, but during all that time no living creature came within range of her. She was on the verge of moving along to another place when a dim movement far across the subsurface clearing caught her attention, and she remained still.

It was a water snake about thirty inches in length, slowly and cautiously winding its sinuous way along the fringe of vegetation, seeking prey. Although it would eventually work its way to within range of the turtle if it continued following this fringe, there was little likelihood that it would itself fall prey to the snapper, since it was a very swift and agile swimmer, its reflexes excellent and its underwater eyesight unusually keen. Nevertheless, the turtle remained rock still and watched its approach.

The snake paused frequently, poking its streamlined head into every possible hiding place it encountered — small hollows in the vegetation and crannies between rocks or under logs. And when it was still eight feet or more distant from the turtle it abruptly started a six-inch bass that had been poised in perfect concealment among the weeds only an inch from the bottom.

Under normal circumstances the bass would have shot away so swiftly that there would have been no opportunity for the snake to catch it, but this particular bass was not well. Just two weeks ago it had been caught by an angler on a worm-baited hook. The hook had not done any serious damage and the fisherman had turned the bass loose, but, in its struggles to escape, the fish had flipped out of his hand and fallen into the bottom of his boat. There it had flopped about furiously and the man had had his hand on it several times and lost it again before finally pinning it to the floor of the boat, grasping it firmly and tossing it back into the water.

In the process of all this, a large swath of the protective mucous covering the fish's body had been scraped away and the flesh near the tail was slightly bruised. Within two days a fuzzy bacterial growth had formed on the spot and begun to spread. And now nearly the entire rear quarter of the fish's right side was diseased and its swimming ability exceedingly hampered.

Startled by the snake, the bass darted out into the open water of the clearing in an attempt to escape, but the water snake instantly assessed its hindered ability and flashed after it. Too late the fish realized its error in streaking into the open and, as best it could, dodged and circled and then tried to get back to the weed cover. Cut off by the snake from this haven, it swam frantically toward the surface, but didn't make it. With impressive swimming skill the snake followed, overtook and finally snatched the fish across its belly only a few inches beneath the surface. And already terribly wearied from its exertions, there was not much struggle left in the sickly fish.

The snake instinctively pulled the little bass back to the bottom. There it could force the head and gills of the fish deep into the sand to suffocate it prior to swallowing it. But this time it didn't happen that way. The pursuit had taken him directly over the motionless turtle, and as they settled not ten inches away, the snapper went into action.

With unbelievable speed her head shot forward with mouth agape, and the fierce jaws snapped closed with the speed and irresistibility of a steel trap over the snake's body only an inch behind the head. The body of the snake writhed furiously and a cloud of sandy silt obscured them. Even though the turtle's jaws had severed the spine and very nearly cut the head clean from the body, the snake's motor reflexes caused it to continue to thrash and whip about help-lessly.

From out of the cloud of silt fogging the clearing the bass emerged, swimming groggily but not badly damaged by the encounter. It angled off into the protective weeds to hide again and regain its strength. But though it had miraculously been re-prieved in this encounter, it could not live long. In the often harsh world of nature, a diseased creature does not long survive. Today it had escaped, but in a short time it would fall prey to a turtle or a larger predatory fish or perhaps even to another snake. And even if it somehow managed to elude them it would soon grow weaker and need to rest increasingly more on the bottom, and eventually a large crayfish would grip it in sharp pincers and quickly sever its gills, and that would be the end.

Back in the clearing the cloud was gradually settling and most movement had ceased. Now and then a faint quiver still ran down the length of the snake's body, but it had died quickly during the frantic struggle and such movement that occurred now was only dwindling muscle reflex action.

The turtle was in no hurry. She retained her hold for ten minutes more before putting on additional pressure with her jaws and completing the job of severing the head. She swallowed the segment remaining in her mouth, picked up the head and swallowed that and then started in on the body. It disappeared down her throat so steadily and smoothly that there was the illusion of the snake crawling inside her of its own accord. In three minutes it was gone.

The meal satisfied the snapper for the time being, and now she pushed herself slowly to the surface and raised her head only above the water. For several minutes she floated there, breathing deeply, and then she submerged again and began a somewhat more purposeful walk along the bottom toward the marsh. It was a long distance to go but, except for surfacing twice to breathe, she moved along at a steady pace and only stopped two times — once to eat a large dead bluegill she came across on the bottom and again to search out and eat a medium-sized dead bullfrog her keen sense of smell had detected floating on the surface. By the time she entered the shallower mucky waters of the marsh it was the twilight of day.

The water in which she chose to rest here was only a foot and a half deep, and she propped her tail and hind legs on the bottom and let her eyes and nose project slightly from the water beside a pile of matted reeds and rushes floating on the surface.

She had not been in this position for ten minutes when there came a clamor of peepings, splashes and quacks as a hen mallard swam into view leading a boisterous platoon of eleven ducklings. They stretched out behind her in ragged single file for six or eight feet and they were all headed directly for the floating mass of vegetation, obviously intent upon using it as a resting place for the night.

They reached it three or four feet from where the turtle was hidden, but she did not move. The adult bird quacked twice and, balancing herself with spread wings, climbed upon the pile. It bobbed some with her weight but held her, and the ducklings followed in a rush, breaking their filelike procession and scrambling toward the natural raft as if it were a beachhead they were assaulting.

One of the babies that made up the trailing foursome of the young platoon found a thick reed root system floating in its way and fluttered its own tiny wings energetically if ineffectually as it clambered over, peeping plaintively all the while. Almost as if it had meant to do so, it swam directly toward the hidden turtle and never even realized its peril until there came that lightninglike thrust of the head and razor-edged jaws crushed its small body.

The hen mallard screamed a warning and thrashed

off the other side of the matted reeds into the tower-
ing cattail cover beyond and the ten remaining ducklings followed her with surprising speed but without
a sound issuing from their mouths.

The turtle stayed where she was, holding the little
duckling just under the surface until its struggling
ceased and then ate it whole and continued her rest
well into the night.

At length, with the sliver of moon already well
past its zenith, she began moving again in a very
determined manner.

XVI

THE TWENTIETH
DAY OF MAY

T HE snapping turtle had a great deal of strength
in her legs and she needed it now to force her
way through the reed growth which became denser
the closer she came to shore. But at last the ground
firmed beneath her, and the water and reeds were
left behind, and she was plowing her way through
deep sedge grass up a slight incline that persisted
for a considerable distance.

Upon reaching the top of it, a hundred yards or
more from the marsh, she paused to rest beside a
fence row. On the other side of the barbed wire fence
was a cornfield where new spears were only now
beginning to break ground. Every year for the past
ten years this was where she had laid her eggs, and
that was her purpose in coming here this night.

She did not, however, always get here at the same time of the year. In some years she had deposited her clutch as early as the middle of April or early May, but normally she laid them during June or July. It took ten full weeks of good hot weather for the eggs to hatch, and if she was late with her laying and the summer was cool, they might well remain in the ground over the winter and not hatch until the following spring — a true case of hibernation within the egg.

Such had been the case last year when she had mated later than any year before — in early August — and her eggs were not deposited, in this very field a little way from where she was right now, until September.

The uphill climb had been exhausting, but now, somewhat refreshed from her pause, she plodded slowly out into the broken earth of the cornfield and did not stop again until she was fully twenty yards from the fence row. Here she turned around in a circle several times and then dug her front claws deep into the ground to maintain a good leverage while her hind feet began to dig with alternate scooping movements. She would bend her foot back on itself, dig the toes in and then move her leg in a semicircle, all the while pushing the foot further down, like an auger, and forming a cup in the webbing of her foot to catch the dirt she had loosened. Carefully then her leg would rise from the hole, move to one side and flip the dirt away, sometimes as far as ten feet from her.

The hole she made was roughly funnel-shaped, perhaps six or seven inches in diameter at the top and a foot in diameter at the bottom. When she had reached a depth of five or six inches she stopped and rested again.

Then the oviduct at the base of her tail began swelling outward and the eggs, singly or in clusters of two or three, were deposited in the hole until a total of twenty-nine had been laid. Each egg was almost perfectly round, just under an inch in diameter and snowy white. More than anything else they looked like wet ping pong balls. The shells were not as hard as those of eggs laid by birds, but instead were like a tough thin parchment which could be dented easily with a little pressure.

As soon as she finished laying, and with the sun just beginning to rise, she commenced refilling the hole with dirt, pushing loose soil toward her rear with her front feet and relaying it to the hole with her rear. It did not take her very long to bury them, and when the earth above the eggs was level with that of the field surrounding the site, she turned several times around over it and scratched drier earth and bits of husk over the top so that when she was finished, someone who had not accurately marked the spot while she was in the act of laying the eggs could not possibly have found them.

The sun was high by the time she began her laborious trek back to the lake, and she was very weary. The land travel, digging and egg-laying were all energy-sapping operations. And she was hungry.

A faint scratching sound caught her attention as she paused briefly to rest before reaching the fence row, and she turned her head to learn its source. She found it at once. Not more than a dozen feet from her a whole clutch of tiny snapping turtles fought their way to the surface and with urgent instinctive haste began scrambling toward the lake.

These were her own offspring — hatchlings from those eggs she had laid so late last season. All winter long, through sub-zero temperatures when the ground had frozen hard, they had lain here. Perhaps they might have hatched sooner than now, but spring plowing had buried them deeper than normal, without injuring them, and it had taken considerably longer for the warmth of the sun to reach and help develop them, to give them the stimulus to break free of their shells, dig their way to the surface and start life on their own.

It is unlikely that the large female turtle remembered this exact spot or recognized these silver-dollar-sized turtles as her own babies. To her, at this time and place, they represented only one thing: food. She increased her speed and reached the site when only slightly more than half had already escaped their prison and scuttled away.

Their shells, rough and wrinkled and barely an inch long, were still very soft, hardly stronger than the shells of the eggs had been. For a day or so they would remain thus, and it was during this period of life that they were the most vulnerable, for any number of predators would devour them with dispatch.

To each was attached a yellowish yolk sac of tough membrane which dragged along below them as they scrambled toward the water. Not until this preliminary food source was consumed — in twenty-four to thirty-six hours — would upper and lower shells begin to take on some degree of hardness.

Their tails were quite long, much longer now in

proportion to their bodies than they would be when the turtles were more mature. As they scampered across the rough ground they whipped these tails from side to side, and this seemed to assist in their locomotion.

As soon as she came within range of them, the head of the female darted out rapidly in a series of strikes and each time it withdrew with a struggling infant turtle gripped tightly. Tiny they may have been, but not without spirit, for even as she held each for a moment before gulping it down, the head of the baby struck repeatedly at her, with instinctive ferociousness.

Once free of the earth, these young were more agile than she, and so it was necessary for her to capture them the exact moment they broke loose. She caught and swallowed nine of them before the activity ceased. And just as she moved to resume her march to the lake, a lone straggler broke loose and began to run. Her head darted out, but she had been caught slightly off balance and the distance was a little too great. The wicked jaws missed the shell and snapped off half the tail with an audible click.

If anything, this made the newly hatched turtle only run the harder. And neither disappointed nor pleased, the big female simply swallowed the section of tail and continued lumbering slowly toward the water.

*   *   *

Though smarting from the loss of his tail, the baby snapping turtle was not seriously injured, but the damage could well have been fatal. Had he been a female he almost assuredly would have died from the injury, for on the female snapping turtle the vent is located closer to the tip of the tail than on the male, and his little tail had been severed only a fraction of an inch behind the vent.

He ran a long way without stopping, and when he did finally stop it was in deep protective grasses where he rested for only a few brief moments at a time and not until he was sure that he had hidden himself well. Hawks, crows, buzzards and herons would not hesitate to snap him up if they saw him, and even though it was daylight there was always the possibility of running afoul of a fox, skunk or raccoon which would make a snack of him without delay. Larger snakes, too, such as the king snakes and pilot blacks, bull snakes or water snakes, would also eat him.

His greatest safety lay in reaching the water and so, even though the overland trip was rough and fatiguing and he was desperately weary, instinct drove him on and would not permit him to stay long in one spot.

He moved quite rapidly for one so little and actually he made the trip back to the first water of the marsh in considerably less time than the adult female was able to. Not more than a half hour after digging his way free from the earth in the cornfield, he was swimming. Not well, perhaps, and certainly not very rapidly, but nonetheless swimming.

The water felt cool and refreshing around him and he submerged gladly, only to bob right back to the surface within a few inches. Not only was the yolk sac a definite drag against him in the water, but it tended to buoy him up and prevent him from getting too near the bottom. Once again the infinite wisdom of nature was evidenced: the more he moved around at this stage of his life, the more apt he was to be seen and caught by some creature, and so the drag created by the yolk sac forced him to stop and rest often; further, in these shallow murky waters the bottom was alive with predators, and so it was a fortunate thing that the yolk sac buoyed him up. Great carp, so large that their broad backs were often exposed above the surface, prowled here, as did huge spotted gars four or five feet in length, their alligatorlike jaws liberally studded with needle-sharp teeth. Even more dangerous were the prehistoric-appearing bowfins, whose sensitive nostrils were constantly seeking out food — great wide-mouthed fish with heavy armor plating and dorsal fins running down almost the entire length of their backs, and so large that even the biggest bass in the lake feared them and gave them a wide berth.

He rested now, his front feet clinging to a bit of drifting vegetation and his little head turning this way and that fearfully. But little by little the fear evaporated and his innate predatory instincts came to the fore. A few inches away from him a large may-fly struggled weakly on the surface in its death throes, and he swam to it at once and gulped it down. He then detected a nymph climbing a reed stalk just below the surface, and he plucked it off and ate it, too.

Slowly, gradually he worked his way out farther in the marsh, and when finally he encountered a little raft of partially submerged reed matting, he crawled onto it until he could rest motionlessly, with all but his head and the uppermost portion of his top shell submerged.

It had been a busy first day of active life for him and he was very tired. And so now, well settled and as safe from predation as he could hope to have been, he slept off and on for the rest of the day and night.

XVII

THE TWENTY - FIRST
DAY OF MAY

B Y midmorning on this bright and pleasant day
the little snapping turtle's yolk sac was all but
absorbed. Though he had taken much sustenance
from it, nevertheless he was hungry and began to
hunt actively again.

He was unusually lucky. After swimming only
twenty feet or so — swimming which was not ad-
versely affected by the loss of his tail and which was,
in fact, quite a bit easier now that the yolk sac was
almost gone — he detected a faint smell of decomposing flesh. The scent was in both the air and water,
and after some experimentation, swimming with his
head in the air to follow the airborne trail, he discovered it was much simpler to follow that same scent

underwater, where the sluggish currents had tended to keep it more concentrated.

Ten feet from where he first detected the scent he found its source. The body of a naked red-winged blackbird floated half hidden beneath a drifting sweet flag leaf. The fact that it was very tiny and still wholly unfeathered and its eyes unopened indicated that it had probably fallen from its nest only a short time after hatching.

Although his beak was far from being as hard or as sharp as it would become in time and he had to labor hard at it, the little snapping turtle nevertheless managed to gnaw off pieces of flesh and swallow them. It was a tedious job but he kept at it persistently and had consumed quite a sizable portion of the bird when suddenly a bubble of gasses escaped from it and it sank. Taking a deep breath, he followed the scent trail it made all the way to the bottom, two feet below.

The little carcass had almost buried itself in the deep loose muck, and he tugged fiercely at it to pull it free. And then, quite unexpectedly, he became alarmed. Perhaps he had detected just the faintest movement of the water; perhaps it was an unfamiliar vibration he caught; perhaps it was an alien scent. Whatever the cause, his instinct drove him to drop the bird's remains at once and hide, and he did so, thrusting himself so deeply into the slime of the bottom that he was buried.

He had been none too soon. A large bluish-black catfish, lured by the same scent that had drawn the little turtle, cruised onto the scene, easily located the torn carcass in the mud and sucked it in as neatly as a vacuum cleaner sucks up a ball of lint. Just as casually the big fish cruised away.

Fifteen minutes later, his air supply dwindling, the little turtle eased his way out of the mud and swam rapidly to the surface. The danger gone, he was no longer concerned about it. But even though he couldn't recognize it as such, the incident had taught him a good lesson: if he could smell food in the water and find it, other creatures could do the same, and such creatures, as this catfish had been, could well be big enough to eat him along with what he had been enticed to eat.

By late afternoon the yolk sac had vanished and his upper shell, while yet by no means very bony, was considerably tougher than it was at this time yesterday. It had now acquired a texture similar to that of a medium-hard leather. In another day or two it would take on a gristly hardness it would retain for many months to come, but not until he was about a

year old would it take on the bone-hard quality it
would maintain for the rest of his life.

Regardless of the fact that the little shell had
hardened to a slight degree, he was still highly vulnerable, and he moved about accordingly, careful to
keep to cover whenever possible, to camouflage himself well when he rested and to keep all his senses
keenly alert for danger.

Just after sunset, upon finishing a two-hour nap,
he approached a tiny island hardly six feet in cir-
cumference. It jutted only two or three inches above
the water and he swam along its edge slowly, inspecting every little niche and miniature cove in the shoreline for possible prey. Equally, he was sharply on the
lookout for any movement which might spell danger
to himself. And that was where he made his single big
mistake.

The danger that loomed for him now was a stationary one.

Half a yard directly ahead of him, with only its
bulging eyes and expansive mouth above water, sat a
tremendous bullfrog. She was eleven years old and
had, in surviving this long, become very wise in the
ways of both predators and prey. She knew, for
example, that it was not an uncommon practice for
young inexperienced hunters like this turtle to care-

fully comb such shorelines for food, and so it was here that she waited for them to come past. A wide variety of creatures — from as small as mayflies and June bugs and spiders to as large as fair-sized fish, smaller bullfrogs, marsh mice and ducklings — had been devoured by this huge frog. In fact, this very morning just before daylight she had caught another bullfrog easily half her own size and gulped it down with only a little difficulty. And though that meal was not yet entirely digested and she was not particularly hungry, still she watched the little turtle's approach with interest.

When the snapper reached the point where he was passing in the small gap between her head and the shore and only two inches separated them, the frog abruptly surged forward and caught him firmly in her mouth.

Futilely the turtle tried to bite his attacker and kicked frantically to get free, but the hold was unbreakable. Using her front feet in the manner of hands, the bullfrog stuffed the little reptile deep into her throat and swallowed him. In a moment she resumed her previous position in the water beside some debris, so well hidden that, except occasionally when she blinked, she was undetectable. It was one of the reasons she had lived so long.

Within her stomach the big female bullfrog could feel the continued movement of the tiny snapping turtle as it sought an escape from its dilemma, but the movement did not bother her. It would very soon grow progressively weaker and then eventually cease altogether as the digestive juices killed the turtle.

And as she floated with her long legs trailing down in the water, a nine-pound largemouth bass that had been attracted by the noise she had made in catching the turtle, poised himself behind her. . . .

EPILOGUE

May is always a beautiful month at Oak Lake. The trees are becoming cloaked in new light green and the marsh has become an emerald sea of reeds. The air is filled with myriad scents and myriad sounds, and the movement of a multitude of wildlife is everywhere.

To the casual onlooker it is a pleasant place — a spot where the cares of life seem to dwindle and become not so demanding. It is a place where flights of ducks come hurtling out of the sky to skid along the water surface in brief planing splashes and then quack contentedly among themselves. It is a place where a fine largemouth bass breaks the mirrorlike surface late in the evening, sending out an ever-expanding pattern of concentric rings. It is a place *where a red-tailed hawk on motionless wings rides air currents effortlessly and with consummate grace for hours at a time, and where the pleasant rumble of bullfrogs is a nightly chorus.*

But this is only the surface appearance — the first page of the prologue to a massive volume which never ends and on whose individual pages the cycles of life among the inhabitants here are chronicled.

It is a volume of nature — a beautiful, constantly moving, constantly changing story of birth and life and death; frequently harsh and oftentimes frightening, but never maliciously cruel.

For in nature's book, everything has its place and its time; there exists a persistent interdependency of its creatures one upon another.

And there is never waste.

There are, amongst the hundreds and thousands of individual stories, many which end in sudden and violent death, but despite this it is a volume with a strange and everlasting timelessness. And there is, over all, a pervading sense of peace.

It is a volume that only God could write.